KW-553-179

Human Rights in the Curriculum

History

a handbook for use in the secondary school classroom

Edited by Sara Slater and Margot Brown
Centre for Global Education
York St John College
York YO31 7EX

with additional contributions from
Margaret Hogg and Pamela Mountford, Huntingdon School, York,
and Joan Storey, Easingwold School.

LIVERPOOL HOPE
UNIVERSITY
LIBRARY
PO BOX 95
LIVERPOOL L16 9LB

LIVERPOOL HOPE UNIVERSITY
Order No./Invoice No. £14.25
L007004583/M1225358
Accession No.
550327
Class No.
372.92T SLA
Control No.
isbn
Catal.
24 7/09

Acknowledgements

Thanks for constructive critical comments to Amanda Gilbert of Rhodesway Upper School, Bradford; Lynn Moran of Bowling Community College, Bradford; Sharyn Robinson of Woodroyd Middle School, Bradford; David Fitch, David Jackson and Julia Kendall of Interfaith Education Centre, Bradford.

For additional material and editing support we thank Valerie Clements, Alison Gurden, Dan Jones, Rose McCausland and Margherita Rendel. For typing the manuscript, thanks to Susan Bainbridge.

First published in 2002 by
Amnesty International UK and the Education in Human Rights Network
© Amnesty International UK, 2002

Amnesty International UK
99-119 Rosebery Avenue
London EC1R 4RE
www.amnesty.org.uk/

ISBN 1 873328 52 4
AIUK product code PB270

This book is one of a series, *Human Rights in the Curriculum*, that aims to provide materials for teaching human rights and responsibilities in secondary schools. Other books in the series cover Geography, Religious Education, English, French and Spanish. The development of this series was supported by a grant from the Community Fund UK (formerly the National Lottery Charities Board).

Contents

Cartoon by Angela Martin

Education in Human Rights Network

The Education In Human Rights Network (EIHRN) was set up in January 1987 to enable and encourage communication between people working in a variety of educational settings who are interested in promoting awareness and understanding of human rights.

The network membership of individuals and organisations meet regularly in London. Member organisations include: Amnesty International UK, the British Institute of Human Rights, the Centre for Global Education, Charter 88, The Bar Human Rights Committee, the Citizenship Foundation, the Council for Education in World Citizenship, the Human Rights Centre at the University of Essex, Anti-Slavery International, Quaker Peace and Social Witness, the Refugee Council, UNICEF, and the Women's International League for Peace and Freedom. Their addresses are listed at the back of this book.

The network has previously co-published with Amnesty International a handbook for teaching about human rights in the primary school: *Our World, Our Rights*. The network also runs an annual summer school and produces a termly newsletter. For more information about the network meetings, summer school and the newsletter please contact the secretary to the network.

EIHRN

Valerie Clements (Secretary),
Quaker Peace and Social Witness Education
Advisory Programme, Friends House,
Euston Road, London NW1 2BJ
Tel: 020 7582 6992
Email: valerie@quaker.org.uk

Amnesty International

Amnesty International is a worldwide, independent, voluntary movement of people working to promote the human rights enshrined in the Universal Declaration of Human Rights, through campaigning, education and pressure on governments to ratify and implement human rights treaties.

It is a democratic, self-governing movement with more than a million members. It is independent of any government, political persuasion or religious creed, and is funded by its membership and by public donations. Its work is based on careful research.

Amnesty International opposes some of the gravest violations by governments of people's civil and political rights. Members work for the release of all prisoners of conscience; for fair and prompt trials for all political prisoners; for the abolition of the death penalty, torture and other ill-treatment of prisoners; for an end to political killings and 'disappearances'. Amnesty calls on armed political groups to respect human rights and to halt abuses such as hostage taking, torture and unlawful killings.

Amnesty International campaigns for human rights through its work with the United Nations and regional intergovernmental organisations. It also works for refugees, on international military, security and police relations, and on economic and cultural relations.

Amnesty International United Kingdom,
99 Rosebery Avenue, London EC1R 4RE
Tel: 020 7814 6200
Email: education@amnesty.org.uk
Website: www.amnesty.org.uk

Introduction

Human rights in the History curriculum

This resource book on history, human rights and related issues has been largely written, trialled in secondary History classrooms and collated by History teachers. Each activity should take about 40 minutes. It is designed for students of History aged 13+. Much of the material could also be used in Religious Education, Modern Studies and PSHE.

The History curricula in the United Kingdom provide many opportunities to study human rights and the surroundings areas of justice, democracy, power, rights, freedom and resolution of conflict. The themed units in this book are not necessarily intended for use as whole programme units of study, but as activities that naturally follow on from one to another. They can be used to complement existing work or stand alone.

In the curricula of Scotland, Northen Ireland and England and Wales, the themes appear as follows:

Slavery

Northern Ireland KS3: Unit 3 *Union to Partition* Part B
England and Wales KS3: National Curriculum: Programmes of Study Unit 3: *Britain 1750 – circa 1900*; A world study before 1900 eg *Black People and the Americas*
Scotland Standard Grade Syllabus: Unit 3: *People and Power (USA 1850 – 1880)* Intermediate Syllabus: *The British Slave Trade and its Abolition*

Child Labour and Working Conditions

Northern Ireland KS3: Programme 3 (A): *Union to Partition* includes social and economic change in Ireland and Britain 1800 to 1922
England and Wales KS3: *Britain 1750 – 1900: The Industrial Revolution* (including legislation to improve working conditions)
Scotland Standard Grade S2: *Industrial Revolution and Child Labour*

Women's Rights

England and Wales KS3: A world study after 1900: *The changing role of women*
Scotland Standard Grade: *Changing Life in Scotland and Britain*

The Holocaust

England and Wales KS3: A world study after 1900, *The Holocaust*
Scotland Standard Grade: *People and Power (Germany 1918-39)*. Intermediate Unit: 3 *The Road to War Germany 1933-9*

Personalities

England and Wales KS3: A world study after 1900: *Roosevelt, Gandhi*

Human Rights

England and Wales KS3: A world study after 1900, *The origins and role of the UN, the UDHR*

1: Human Rights Education

Human rights

Human rights are about treating all people with the equal dignity that they are entitled to as human beings. Every person in the world, including children, must be recognised as having the same worth and dignity without regard to such differences as ethnic origin, colour of skin, sex or beliefs. Working out what this principle means in terms of individual entitlements and needs has arguably been the most important moral advance of recent history.

The United Nations and regional international bodies such as the Council of Europe (of which the United Kingdom is a member) have drafted human rights codes that governments everywhere are urged to implement. National and international institutions have been created to promote and defend human rights. Non-governmental organisations (NGOs) work to uphold human rights standards and campaign against violations of rights. Such organisations include Amnesty International, Anti-Slavery International, Charter 88, Save the Children, UNICEF, the Refugee Council and the United Nations Association.

The best known source of modern thinking about human rights and fundamental freedoms is the Universal Declaration of Human Rights (UDHR) adopted by the General Assembly of the UN on 10 December 1948. This document was the first to proclaim the universality of human rights and to list them in categories of civil, cultural, economic, social and political rights and freedoms. It now forms part of the International Bill of Human Rights which includes two legally binding covenants covering all these categories of rights.

The UDHR proclaims the equal importance of all rights and their interdependence. The struggle to eliminate torture and discrimination and the fight against poverty, hunger, illiteracy and disease, are different parts of the same campaign to secure the needs of all human beings for freedom, security and dignity. Achieving development and securing all human rights are now seen as interdependent goals.

In the United Kingdom the latest step to make rights effective at home comes with the Human Rights Act, 1998. This means that everyone in Britain can now invoke the rights and freedoms in the European Convention on Human Rights before the courts.

Dear Teacher,

I am a survivor of a concentration camp.

My eyes saw what no man should witness:

Gas chambers built by learned engineers.

Children poisoned by educated physicians.

Infants killed by trained nurses.

Women and babies shot and burned by high school and college graduates.

So I am suspicious of education.

My request is: Help your students become human. Your efforts must never produce learned monsters, skilled psychopaths, educated Eichmanns. Reading, writing, arithmetic are important only if they serve to make our children more human.

Letter pinned on a noticeboard

Reflections on citizenship and human rights education

> 'A healthy society is made up of people who care about the future – people who willingly contribute to its development for the common good – people who reject the "don't care" culture, who are not always asking "What's in it for me?" – people who want to be practising citizens. Before this can happen they need to have a sense of belonging – of identity – with the community around them ... Our goal is to create a nation of able, informed and empowered citizens who, on the one hand, know, understand and can enforce their rights; and, on the other, recognise that the path to greatest personal fulfilment lies through active involvement in strengthening their society.
>
> Citizenship education must give people confidence to claim their rights and challenge the *status quo* while, at the same time, make plain that with rights come obligations. It should foster respect for law, justice and democracy. It should nurture concern for the common good at the same time as it encourages independence of thought. It should provide people with an armoury of essential skills; listening, arguing, making a case; and accepting the greater wisdom or force of an alternative view.'
>
> *(Lord Irvine addressing the Citizenship Foundation, 1998. Quoted in The Crick Report.)*

Human rights education has been defined as the combination of knowledge about rights and responsibilities and the values and skills to put them into action. Its goal is to sensitise students to the rights of others, and to encourage responsible action in safeguarding the rights of all in school and in the wider world.

Human rights education is built on key values underpinning responsible action. They are universally agreed through the declarations and conventions that make up human rights law. It also makes explicit those aspects of daily life where rights and responsibilities are secure and protected, or where they are infringed, in the UK and elsewhere. In schools this is seen through the ethos and management of the school, its policies towards pupils, staff, governors and visitors.

Human rights education is also explicit in the taught curriculum. Each subject area contains elements which aid an understanding of rights and responsibilities. Human rights education develops skills for participation in wider society. In schools where rights and responsibilities form the framework for learning, pupils experience democracy in action.

The curriculum changes introduced in September 2000 now include citizenship education as a statutory requirement for KS3 and KS4. There are similar changes taking place in Scotland, with the Scottish office introducing new Guidelines on Education for Citizenship. Citizenship education 'contributes to the school curriculum by giving pupils the knowledge, understanding and skills to enable them to participate in society as active citizens of our democracy. It enables them to be informed, critical and responsible and aware of their *duties and rights*'. (The Secretary of State's Proposals, 1999: 28. Our emphasis). Citizenship education is part of human rights education.

Education for Citizenship and Teaching of Democracy in Schools (the Crick Report) is the final report of the Advisory Group on Citizenship and forms the basis of the new Citizenship Orders. It identifies the essential elements which pupils should have experienced by the end of schooling. These include key concepts of 'democracy and autocracy; equality and diversity; fairness, justice, the rule of law and human rights; rights and responsibilities'. Values and dispositions include 'belief in human dignity and equality; determination to act justly; commitment to equal opportunities and gender equality; and concern for human rights'. Skills and aptitudes include 'ability to recognise forms of manipulation and persuasion; ability to consider and appreciate the experience and perspective of others; and the ability to identify, respond to and influence social, moral and political challenges and situations'. Finally, the knowledge and understanding includes 'legal and moral rights and responsibilities of individuals and communities; the rights and responsibilities of citizens as consumers, employers and family and community members; and human rights charters and issues' (Crick Report, 1998: 44).

Dealing with prejudice and discrimination

Important though the Crick Report is in putting human rights education into the National Curriculum as part of a new statutory curriculum subject, it does not deal adequately with prejudice and discrimination in society. As Professor Audrey Osler, previously secretary of EIHRN, outlines in *Citizen* (Autumn/ Winter 1999): 'Racism has been identified by a number of international organisations, including the European Commission and the Council of Europe, as one of the forces which serves to undermine democracy in Europe, and one which therefore should be addressed through Education programmes. Effectively, racism acts as a barrier to citizenship.' She points out that this is not addressed in the Crick Report.

The MacPherson Report on the Stephen Lawrence Inquiry, which was published after Crick and before the new curriculum, states: 'If racism is to be eradicated there must be specific and co-ordinated action both within the agencies themselves and by society at large, particularly through the education system, from pre-primary school upwards and onwards.'

Human rights education with its focus on equality, justice and human dignity and its concern for taking responsibility is ideally placed to contribute to classroom work which identifies racism where it occurs, develops understanding of what racism is and contributes to skills to challenge the prejudice and discrimination which racism generates.

Osler writes that: 'In Britain anti-racism is often seen simply as the opposite of racism, rather than a set of values or beliefs which are part of the human rights discourse. ... An understanding of racism, the ways in which it serves to undermine democracy, and the skills to challenge this anti-democratic force, are essential features of any education programme which seeks to promote the political literacy of young people.'

Human rights education is about respecting fundamental values. One reservation, in addition to that expressed by Osler, is that certain groups in society are not included in citizenship and its focus on democratic participation. These include, for example, asylum-seekers, homeless people, and Traveller communities. We would advocate therefore that human rights education reaches those parts which citizenship education does not.

Professor Margherita Rendel writes: 'The *Speaker's Report on Citizenship* quotes the Hansard Society's position that teaching citizenship should encourage tolerance and respect for individuals and their property, irrespective of a person's gender, race, culture or religion ... [and] encourage young people to behave honourably and with integrity...' (1998). The *Speaker's Report* and curriculum documents note the importance of providing challenging work in citizenship and human rights for all pupils.

Human rights means respect for all human beings including those who are different and those who are disadvantaged whether they are, for example, asylum-seekers, homeless, Travellers, in poverty, gay or elderly or those with disabilities. Human rights include respect for living things, the natural and human made environment. EIHRN advocates that education for citizenship should address all forms of discrimination and inequality.

The Citizenship Advisory Group pointed out in 1999 that citizenship education 'was about overcoming structural barriers to equality: challenging racism and sexism...'.

Sexism is unjust and also a danger to 51 per cent of the population. It is welcome that girls and young women are now doing well in education, but much discrimination remains in employment and in society. Recent research has shown that nearly 25 per cent of young men thought it was all right to hit a woman if she had slept with someone else and 10 per cent thought so if she had been 'disrespectful'.*

The need to address homophobia, whatever opinion may be held about homosexuality, lies behind the attempt to repeal the notorious Section 28. Too often those with disabilities, elderly people, refugees or asylum-seekers are wrongly assumed to have nothing to contribute to society; Travellers and those in poverty too often do not receive the good education they deserve. Members of these groups are as a result likely to be excluded from effective citizenship and denied their human rights.

These issues are included either expressly or by implication or by the links to other subjects in the National Curriculum.

**S Burton and J Kitzinger et al, 1998, Young People's Attitudes Towards Violence, Sex and Relationships, Zero Tolerance Charitable Trust (Edinburgh).*

Teaching and learning about human rights

Values

- Human dignity (pupils develop a sense of worth of self and others, irrespective of social, cultural, ethnic, linguistic or faith background)
- Justice and fairness (pupils value genuinely democratic processes and principles and are willing to take action on this)
- Commitment to equality (pupils recognise the principle of equality underpinning relationships between individuals, groups and societies)
- Appreciation of diversity (pupils develop an open-minded approach to other cultures and social groups and are willing to learn from them).

Skills

- Communication (reading, written and oral expression, discussion, debate, listening)
- Using the tools of the discipline (eg reading and interpreting maps, charts, graphs, reference materials, visual literacy)
- Critical thinking (collecting, analysing material from multiple sources, identifying different perspectives; distinguishing between fact and opinion, detecting prejudice, bias, omission; reaching logical, fair, balanced conclusions)
- Social skills (cooperation, conflict resolution, mediation, forming positive relationships).

Knowledge

- Understanding concepts – equality, human dignity, non-discrimination, democracy and universality
- Understanding how human rights appear in one's own life and in the lives of others elsewhere in the world, today and in the past. Exploring how they might look in the future
- Understanding that human rights may be experienced differently by different groups within the same society – in the UK and elsewhere
- Understanding that human rights give a framework for agreed standards of behaviour in school, in the community, nationally and globally
- Understanding who supports or protects human rights – individuals, organisations, national and international law
- Knowing about the major international instruments – such as the Universal Declaration of Human Rights (1948), UN Convention on the Rights of the Child (1989)
- Understanding why these international documents came about and how they affect daily lives in the UK and elsewhere in the world.

Controversial issues

- A controversial issue is an issue about which there is no single fixed or universally held point of view
- Sometimes the right of one person/group is in direct conflict with the right of others
- Recognising bias and evaluating evidence contributes to a balanced approach to issues
- Controversial issues are important in themselves and help pupils learn about the wider world
- Controversial issues are often major issues of the day over which young people are struggling to find an answer
- Controversial issues can be moral, ethical, economic, political, cultural, religious, social, environmental and technological. They can affect young people locally, nationally or globally
- Controversial issues can contribute to the development of:
  - willingness and empathy to perceive and understand the interests, beliefs and viewpoints of others
  - willingness and ability to apply reasoning skills to problems and to value a respect for truth and evidence in forming or holding opinions
  - willingness and ability to participate in decision-making, to value freedom, to choose between alternatives, and to value fairness as a basis for making and judging decisions
- Controversial issues are often sensitive issues on which pupils – and teachers – hold strong opinions.

Adapted from the Crick Report (1998)

A human rights school?

It is not only in the formal curriculum that human rights have a place in school. Schools spend much time and effort in creating a safe yet invigorating learning environment. This is achieved not only through the dedication and vision of individual teachers working in individual classrooms, but also through all members of the school community working together towards common goals. Human rights values can provide a framework to help schools develop an ethos which respects the rights of all, and responds positively to the responsibilities this brings.

A checklist for teaching and learning

A human rights school:

- Encompasses a range of learning styles, from instruction, through group work, to well structured opportunities for individual study which teach life-long learning styles
- Encourages group discussion activities around rights issues
- Allows pupils to learn how to work together and respect the rights of others
- Uses a language of rights and allows this vocabulary to be used and practised. Includes words such as:

citizenship	justice	community
loyalty	democracy	participation
dignity	protection	duty
respect	equality	responsibility
fairness	security	

- Incorporates teaching about human rights into subject curricula, giving a living context to rights
- Includes peer mediation, conflict resolution and democratic participation
- Encourages students to identify with the ideal of universal human rights protection. With an inherent belief in fairness, pupils readily respond to the notion that everyone in the classroom has the same rights, including the teacher, and that they must all respect one another's rights. This can counteract cynicism about their own institution.

Planning human rights learning

When planning to include human rights explicitly in the curriculum:

- Identify human rights themes in a unit of work, such as poverty in this country and elsewhere. Poverty has long been recognised as a major abuse of human rights. It infringes Article 25 of the Universal Declaration of Human Rights (UDHR), and generates infringements of rights relating to health, education or physical security
- Develop knowledge and understanding about human rights
- Develop the skills that individuals need to be powerful but sensitive advocates for their own rights and those of others. Develop also the ability to identify, and then take, appropriate action
- Create a school ethos and classroom management based on justice and democracy
- Consider an appropriate range of teaching strategies for the learning needs of all
- Think action! This may mean developing a strategy to reduce bullying and anti-social behaviour in school; it may mean fund-raising for a particular organisation or cause; it may mean students undertaking an awareness-raising assembly; writing to a prisoner of conscience, an organisation or MP; or involvement in the local community. It may also mean changing the students' own behaviour towards others in home or school.

A human rights school ethos

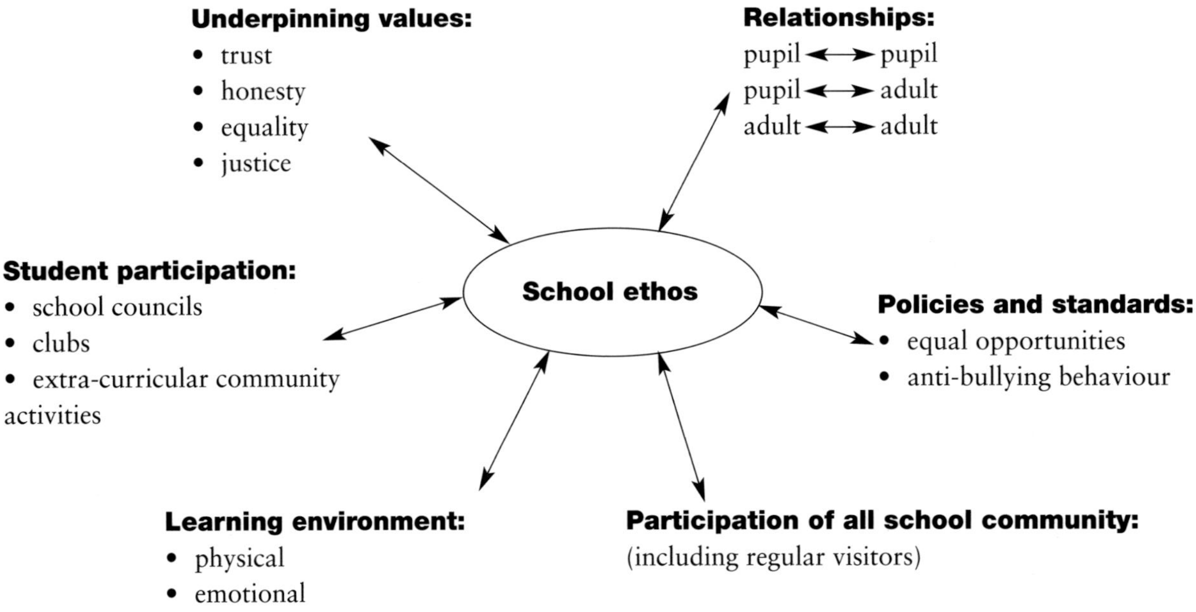

2: Classroom Activities

ACTIVITY

Teachers' notes

ACTIVITY 1 Launching into human rights

Aim:
To introduce some examples of articles in the Universal Declaration of Human Rights (UDHR) and the Convention on the Rights of the Child (CRC), and their infringement. The situations which students consider are real events, and reflect a mixture of home, school, local community and global contexts.

Time:
40 minutes

Materials:
- One photocopy of the Story Sheets for each group of four students (pages 15 and 16)
- One copy of the UDHR and CRC for each group (pages 68-71)
- One photocopy of the Human Rights Grid for each group (page 17)
- One copy of the Remedies Sheet for each group (page 18)*

What to do:
- Give each group the Story Sheets, a copy of the UDHR, the CRC and a copy of the grid.
- Ask the students to read the stories and check with the UDHR to see which articles are being infringed. For some stories there may be more than one violation. Students should write the numbers of the article(s) violated in the appropriate box on the grid.
- Ask each group to nominate a speaker who will explain why they chose certain articles for one of the stories. Each group takes turns until each story has been discussed. Draw out similarities and differences between the groups. (For ease of identification key words are in bold in the stories.)

OR
- Once the groups have completed their grid, ask the students to number off 1-6. All students who numbered 'one' make a new group, all those who are 'two', 'three' or 'four' do likewise.
- The new groups sit with one of the completed grids and the member of the group who took part in filling in that grid explains the reasons for the choice of articles to the others.
- After a short time (three-four minutes), the groups move on to sit with another completed grid. The process is repeated with a different student giving the explanation.
- Continue this until each group has looked at each grid. (This numbering assumes a class of about 30. Alter the number of groups as needed.)

It is important that students realise there are a range of possible remedies for violations of human rights.
- Hand out the Remedies Sheet to each group and ask them to identify which remedy or remedies might be most appropriate for each scenario. Write the remedy number in the appropriate box on the grid.
- Once the students have discussed the remedies, ask them to sort the remedies according to actions the students can take and action to be taken by others. Are they solutions?

* You will find a useful glossary on page 76.

Possible answers to exercise

A UDHR 5, 9. CRC 40
B UDHR 1, 2, 26. CRC 2, 23, 28
C UDHR 23
D UDHR 5. CRC 19, 27, 37, 39
E UDHR 5, 19. CRC 13, 14, 29
F UDHR 2,5,18,26. CRC 2, 14, 17, 28, 30, 37
G UDHR 12. CRC 16
H UDHR 4. CRC 32
I UDHR 1,2. CRC 2
J UDHR 27. CRC 31
K UDHR 1, 2, 16
L UDHR 27. CRC 13, 17, 28, 30

Photocopy original © Amnesty International UK

ACTIVITY 1 Launching into human rights

Story Sheet 1

A.
In Turkey a **12-year-old girl** was **arrested** because the police thought she had stolen some bread. She was hit by the police in the car on the way to the station, was then blindfolded and hurt by more officers. She was kept in the police station for five days and was not allowed to see her mother.

B.
Kerry is 14 and has just moved to a new school in Wales. She is **HIV-positive**. She doesn't tell many people because **they often treat her badly if they know**. Sometimes she is ill and has to have time off school.

C.
In 2000 a café in Scotland was paying adults a wage of £3.70 per hour, but paid the teenagers who had summer jobs there only £2.00 per hour. The adults and the teenagers were doing **exactly the same jobs**.

D.
On 29 April 1998 English newspapers reported that a **12-year-old boy** was repeatedly **beaten up** and physically tortured by **his parents**. His ribs and jaw were broken and he sustained multiple injuries to the rest of his body. This occurred over a period of three weeks while they had him tied to a stair banister.

E.
In 1990 a 13-year old Buddhist nun in Lhasa, Tibet, waved a small flag for five minutes and demanded Tibet's independence from China. She was **jailed** for four months. In 1992 she was **jailed** for another protest. Her **sentence was trebled** when she smuggled a secretly taped song out of prison. In 1996 she shouted 'Free Tibet'. She was **beaten** and her sentence was lengthened to 18 years.

F.
A young Sikh published his account of regular **verbal and physical harassment** he experienced in seven years of school in England. Much was directed at **his long hair and turban**, Sikh sacred symbols. Sometimes teachers would join in or even initiate the jokes. He said it eroded his self-confidence and capacity to concentrate on learning.

Photocopy original © Amnesty International UK

ACTIVITY

ACTIVITY 1 Launching into human rights

Story Sheet 2

G.
A mother, worried about her teenage daughter, **reads her diary**.

H.
In Pakistan Pupo Koli, his wife and eight children were **sold as slaves**. They were made to wear leg-irons in the fields and squat at wooden posts before being chained for the night. For food, they were given flour in such small quantities that for several days every month they ate grass.

I.
A teacher notices that a female student is doing particularly well with a project he has set for the rest of the class. He encourages one of the male students by saying 'Come on Tom ... you don't want to be **beaten by a girl** do you? Now buck up!'

J.
The shops, theatres and galleries in a Welsh town are **not accessible** to people who have a disability or are old and require a wheelchair.

K.
In Japan Buraku people are often **discriminated against** for historical reasons. A young man became engaged to a young woman. Her family investigated the young man's background and found that he came from a Buraku family. They **stopped the wedding**. The young man became very depressed and committed suicide. (Buraku people used to have the job of dealing with dead animals.)

L.
The Berber people are the original people in the country now known as Morocco. A young boy tells of being **forbidden to speak the Berber language in school**. There are almost no examples of Berber culture in school textbooks.

Photocopy original © Amnesty International UK

ACTIVITY 1 Launching into human rights

The Human Rights Grid

Read the stories and find out which articles of the Universal Declaration of Human Rights and the Convention on the Rights of the Child are being abused. There may be more than one article being abused in each situation. Write the numbers of the articles in the corresponding lettered box.

A. **Articles:** **Remedies**	**B.** **Articles:** **Remedies**	**C.** **Articles:** **Remedies**	**D.** **Articles:** **Remedies**
E. **Articles:** **Remedies**	**F.** **Articles:** **Remedies**	**G.** **Articles:** **Remedies**	**H.** **Articles:** **Remedies**
I. **Articles:** **Remedies**	**J.** **Articles:** **Remedies**	**K.** **Articles:** **Remedies**	**L.** **Articles:** **Remedies**

ACTIVITY

Photocopy original © Amnesty International UK

ACTIVITY 1 Launching into human rights

Remedies Sheet

1. Write to the foreign country's High Commissioner or Ambassador in the UK, complaining of the violation.	**2.** Write to the government complaining of the violation and asking for action.
3. Take the problem to the School Council.	**4.** Bring an action in the UK courts under the Human Rights Act for violation of a civil right.
5. Bring a complaint to the European Court of Human Rights (but only after British courts or tribunals have failed).	**6.** Write to your local MP or local councillor highlighting the problems and requesting their assistance.
7. Write to a newspaper to highlight the violation.	**8.** Raise funds for organisations that are working to improve the situation.
9. Find a neutral person to mediate and help to find a solution.	**10.** Educate others on the importance of rights and responsibilities and the problems caused by violations of rights.
11. Organise a petition.	**12.** Make a complaint to the Disability Rights Commission/Equal Opportunities Commission/Commission for Racial Equality.

Photocopy original © Amnesty International UK

Teachers' notes

Slavery past and present

ACTIVITY 2 The Transatlantic Slave Trade

ACTIVITY

Aim:
To encourage students to think about what they already know about the slave trade, as well as some more general human rights issues. Students are also asked to consider black role models in today's society. In this lesson 'black' refers to those African people whose human rights were violated during the Transatlantic Slave Trade.

Time:
40 minutes

Materials:
- One Question Sheet for each student (page 20)
- One Answer Sheet as an overhead transparency (page 21)
- Space for students to move around easily

What to do:
- Explain to the students that they are going to ask each other the questions on the sheet.
- They can do this only when they are out of their chairs and moving around the room.
- They may ask only one question of each student and can answer only one question in return.
- When each member of a pair has answered one question asked by the other, they split up and find another partner to ask, and reply to, a new question.
- When time is up or several students have finished – whichever is sooner – call 'stop' and ask all students to sit down.
- Ask the class to share their answers and compare these with the Answer Sheet. This sheet is not comprehensive and you may well receive good answers not included in this book.
- Students can add to or amend their answers as they listen to the feedback.

Discussion:
- In debriefing on the activity, ask which were the easiest and the most difficult questions to find answers for. Why? Which questions had global/national answers?
- Students could identify the abuses of human rights in their answers, and match them up with articles of the Universal Declaration of Human Rights (UDHR) on pages 68 and 69. Similarly, students could identify which articles in the International Convention on the Elimination of All Forms of Racial Discrimination (CERD) on pages 74 and 75 are sustained and promoted in their answers.
- If the students had any problems in answering a question, set this as research homework.
- Students research for, and produce a poster/report/presentation on one of the organisations/persons/situations on their sheet.

Photocopy original © Amnesty International UK

ACTIVITY

ACTIVITY 2 The Transatlantic Slave Trade

Question Sheet

1.
Name two British ports famous during the Transatlantic Slave Trade.

2.
Slavery has existed throughout history and still exists today. True or false?

3.
How many Africans were taken to the Americas to work as slaves?

4.
Why was the Transatlantic Slave Trade known as the Triangular trade?

5.
Name a black civil rights activist.

6.
What rights were slaves denied?

7.
Name a film that deals with slavery in the US.

8.
Why were slaves branded (scarred with a red-hot iron)?

9.
Name the main types of work that slaves were forced to do.

10.
Name a country where you think that slavery still exists.

11.
What does abolition mean?

12.
Name an organisation that opposes slavery.

How would you put an end to slavery? (Collect as many different suggestions as possible.)

Photocopy original © Amnesty International UK

ACTIVITY 2 The Transatlantic Slave Trade

Answer Sheet

1. Liverpool Bristol	**2.** True. Forced labour and bonded labour are and have been two forms of slavery that exist in many countries around the world.	**3.** Estimated at 15 million. (Many perished in the Middle Passage.)
4. Because the trade route from Europe, to Africa, on to the Americas and back to Europe formed a triangle. 'Goods' were traded at each point of the triangle.	**5.** Martin Luther King Rosa Parks Frederick Douglass Harriet Tubman Sojourner Truth	**6.** The right to marry whom they wished. The right to their own name. Protection from violence and sexual abuse. The right to a family. The right to education. The right to freedom. The right to a fair trial.
7. Amistad Roots The Color Purple Beloved	**8.** The brand showed the initials of the person who 'owned' the slave. If a slave escaped this was a way of identifying to whom they belonged and that they were a slave.	**9.** Domestic work – cooking/cleaning/serving/child-care. Plantation work – working in the fields/looking after animals/processing sugar and cotton.
10. There are more countries where slavery does exist than where it does not. Those where it exists include: the UK; USA; Nepal; Sudan; Thailand; Brazil.	**11.** To end or stop. It comes from the word abolish.	**12.** Anti-Slavery International, Save the Children, UNICEF, Christian Aid, International Labour Organisation, Trades Union Congress.

Use answers to the last question to open up discussion and debate.

Photocopy original © Amnesty International UK

Teachers' notes

ACTIVITY 3 Slavery today

Aim:
To help raise awareness of present day slavery. Many believe that slavery stopped with the end of the Transatlantic Slave Trade, but this is not so. During the Transatlantic Slave Trade, slavery was legal, and it was common to see slaves working in people's homes and on their plantations. Today slavery is illegal, and as a result slavery has become a hidden problem. Now slaves work behind closed doors, in people's houses, in remote rural areas, and in hidden factories.

Time:
40 minutes

Materials:
- One overhead transparency of the Quotations sheet (page 23)
- One or more copies of each Case Study Card, (so that each group of four to six students has one case study (page 24)
- Three Work Cards (page 25)
- A piece of string approximately one and a half metres long or a piece of chalk to draw a line

What to do:

Match the quotes:
- Show the Quotations transparency (answers covered).
- Ask the class which date matches which quotation. Encourage them to say why they have chosen that date and what they think is happening. Is there consensus in the class?
- Now reveal the answers. **In fact all these quotes are from the 1990s.** What is their response? Encourage discussion. If anyone has used the word 'civilised', ask what is meant by 'civilised' in this context.
- Now distribute one Case Study Card to each group of four to six students.

Exploitation line:
- Draw a line on the floor (or use string). At one end place the 'Legal work' card and at the other the 'Slavery' card (you may think of more appropriate wording).
- Divide the class into four groups. Each group is given one of the case studies. After reading it carefully they must choose where to place it on the 'Exploitation line'.
- When every group has placed their case study on the floor, each study is read out in turn.

Discussion:
- Does everyone agree that the case studies are in the right place? Why/why not?
- Draw out students' thoughts on why one situation is better or worse than another. Focus their minds on the rights of the individuals in the case studies. Emphasise that there is no correct way of placing the case studies; different people will have different opinions.
- Can the group decide what elements need to be present to make someone a slave? Examples: no pay, no time off, physical/mental abuse, no freedom to leave work.
- Can the group find relevant articles in the Universal Declaration of Human Rights and/or the Convention on the Rights of the Child that need to be respected/protected to ensure that people are not forced into slavery?

Source: Rose McCausland, Anti-Slavery International.

Photocopy original © Amnesty International UK

ACTIVITY 3 Slavery today

Quotations

Match these quotations to a date

A
Even for a day, if one of us remains absent due to illness or any other reason, they come to our house, drag us out and beat us on the road.

B
I will cut your face. I will kill you and scatter your pieces in the desert if you ever disobey an order. You are my slave. You will do exactly what I say.

C
I have been serving his family since the time of his grandfather and since he was not even born. The owner is younger than me, so I become angry when he abuses or beats me, but there is nobody to take my side. Being helpless, I remain silent.

D
I fear if I stop the work they will kill my relatives and me, they will burn our house.

1. c.1500 BC **2.** 1450 **3.** 1680 **4.** 1990

In fact all these quotes are from the 1990s

ACTIVITY

Photocopy original © Amnesty International UK

ACTIVITY

ACTIVITY 3 Slavery today

Case Studies

Photocopy the page on to card, and cut along the lines.

Case Study 1

Alice is 27 and is from the Philippines. She is a qualified civil engineer and came to London to look for a well-paid job to help pay for her two younger brothers to go to school. When she arrived she could only find live-in domestic work. She has lived and worked for the same family for four years now. She is on call 24 hours a day, cooking, cleaning, washing and doing any odd job. She is not allowed to leave the house and has not had a day's holiday since she started the job.

The family does not pay her cash; instead they have told her that the money she is owed is being paid into an account for her, which she can access when she leaves. On average, Alice has four or five hours sleep and one meal a day. She is constantly tired, and when she makes mistakes her mistress hits her with an old broom. She wants to run away, but is scared and doesn't know who to turn to for help.

Case Study 2

Bhago is 10 years old and lives in India. For the last four years he has been working in a factory making carpets. He lives in the factory with eight other children. They work, eat and sleep in one dark and dusty room and Bhago has a constant cough. The work starts at 6am, and finishes around 9pm.

He has friends in the factory, but they never have time to play. If they talk to one another, the factory owner punishes them. If they make mistakes they get beaten. He misses his family. His father trusted the man who came to their village and offered to take Bhago to a nearby town to give him an education, and teach him how to weave carpets. But he hasn't seen the man, or Bhago, or any of Bhago's wages since. He had hoped that the money Bhago earned could pay for his sister's education. He does not have enough money to travel to the town to look for his son.

Case Study 3

When Mary was eight, she left her family to live with distant relatives in a city hundreds of miles from her village in Togo, West Africa. The agreement was that Mary would receive an education, and in return would help around the house. But Mary has never been to school and rarely leaves her new home.

She is up early every morning and works for 14-16 hours a day. She does all the work around the house, including the cooking, washing, cleaning, and looking after the three children, aged between two and nine. She sleeps on the kitchen floor, and is only allowed to eat the family's leftover food, so sometimes she goes hungry. She doesn't get paid. She has no friends in the city, and longs to return to her village, but when she asks about her family she is told to forget about them.

Case Study 4

Alfredo is 18 and lives in north-east Brazil. There is high unemployment in his town, and so he happily accepted work on an estate in the Amazon, many thousands of miles from his home.

He and 29 other young men travelled by truck for four days to reach the estate. When they arrived, they were told that they owed the estate manager money for their transport. They also had to buy tools, work clothes, hammocks and food from the estate store, which led to even bigger debts.

Alfredo worked hard, clearing trees and undergrowth, so the land could be used for farming, but every week he was told that his wages had gone to paying off his debt at the estate store. Two of his fellow workers confronted the estate manager and demanded their wages, but instead of receiving payment, they were tied up in a room for two weeks and beaten every day. Armed guards patrol the estate, so it is almost impossible to run away. Alfredo knows it is at least a day's walk to the nearest village, and he could easily get lost in the forest.

Photocopy original © Amnesty International UK

ACTIVITY 3 Slavery today

Work Cards

Photocopy the page on to card, and cut along the lines.

Legal work
Slavery
Exploitation line

Photocopy original © Amnesty International UK

Teachers' notes

ACTIVITY

ACTIVITY 4 Slavery: Young miners

Aim:
To open up a discussion about child labour during the period of industrialisation. The drawing on the page opposite (page 27) is from the 1842 Mines Report to the British Parliament. When seen as a whole it is clear that it shows a child pulling a cart in a mineshaft. This simple and quick activity also requires co-operation between group members.

Time:
15 minutes; more with follow-up suggestions

Materials:
- One copy of the picture (page 27) for each group of students
- Cut across the photocopies from scissor symbol to scissor symbol and place each complete set of parts into an envelope, like pieces of a jigsaw

What to do:
- Arrange the class into groups of three or four around a desk.
- Give each group one piece of the 'jigsaw' from the envelope.
- Each group marks two columns on a piece of paper. Head one column 'What we agree about' and the other 'What we are not sure about'.
- Under each heading, the group records all the items they see on their piece of 'jigsaw'. They can then ask for a second piece.
- They place the two pieces together and see if the additional information leads to any changes. They make the changes.
- Add any new information in the appropriate column.
- Repeat with the third jigsaw piece.
- Give a title to the picture.

Discussion:
- What is happening in this drawing? (Several different opinions may be given here.)
- When you saw the first piece what did you think was happening?
- What did you think the boy was doing?
- Why do you think that children are used for this particular job? How old does he look to you?
- How do you think it would feel for the child? Exciting at first? Frightening? Claustrophobic?

Follow-up activities:
- Ask students to look at the Convention on the Rights of the Child (pages 70 and 71). Which rights are being infringed through child labour?
- Give written accounts from child workers (historical or in the present day) to read.
- Ask students to write a diary entry for a child working in the mineshaft; describe their working day and how they would feel about working in such conditions.
- Ask students in small groups to list acceptable and unacceptable jobs for children to do. Share these opinions with the rest of the class.
- For homework, ask students to find out about the types of work done by children around the period of industrialisation. Ask students to present their findings to the rest of the class, and hand in some written evidence of their research next lesson.

Photocopy original © Amnesty International UK

ACTIVITY

ACTIVITY 4 Slavery: Young miners

© BEAMISH The North of England Open Air Museum

Photocopy original © Amnesty International UK

ACTIVITY

Teachers' notes

ACTIVITY 5 Different medical opinions

Aim:
To allow pupils to consider the content and implications of two pieces of historical evidence. With hindsight, it is easy to be critical of the conditions in which children were expected to work but there were conflicting opinions at the time, just as there are conflicting opinions about health issues today.

Time:
40-45 minutes

Materials:
- One copy of the Interview Sheet for each pair of students (page 29)
- One copy of the Question Sheet for each pair (page 30)

What to do:
- Ask each pair to choose to read questions or answers for Dr Whatton's interview and to read it to one another taking the appropriate role.
- Ask them to read Dr Smith's interview, reversing the roles.
- Pairs then work together to fill in the Question Sheet. They link up with another pair and compare results.

Photocopy original © Amnesty International UK

ACTIVITY 5 Different medical opinions

Interview Sheet

Read these interviews with two medical doctors who were asked about the health risks to children working in factories. Remember these are both genuine *sources* of historical evidence. What might not be genuine is what was said during the interviews!

Dr William Whatton worked as a doctor in Manchester.

A committee of the House of Lords chaired by Lord Kenyon interviewed him on 25 May 1818.

Q: Have you had an opportunity of observing whether the work of the children tends to produce bad health among them? Have you observed any particular symptoms of disease about the children?
A: No, I cannot say that I did.

Q: If a child was of a delicate constitution, would you think 12 hours was too long to keep him at work?
A: The labour is so moderate it can scarcely be called labour at all; and under those circumstances I should not think there would be any injury from it.

Q: Do you happen to know whether or not any particular effect is produced upon a child's frame that is kept standing longer than his strength will permit, or rather, than he ought to be subjected to?
A: I am not aware of any effect.

Q: If a child is kept standing longer than his strength will permit, it will produce a diseased affection of the sinews of the knee?
A: I have never seen that.

Dr Samuel Smith worked as a doctor in Leeds.

Michael Sadler MP interviewed him on 16 July 1832.

Q: Is the appearance of factory children easy to be distinguished from that of the children composing the rest of the labouring population differently employed?
A: Yes. It is easy to see that they have not that healthy appearance, they appear languid, weak, and debilitated.

Q: Is not the labour in mills and factories 'light and easy'?
A: It is often described as such, but I do not agree at all with that definition. The exertion required from them is considerable, and, in all instances with which I am acquainted, the whole of their labour is performed in a standing position.

Q: What are the effects of this on the children?
A: By long continued standing the knees become so weak that they turn inwards, producing that deformity which is called 'knock knees' and I have sometimes seen it so striking that the individual has actually lost 12 inches of his height.

Q: Are there many accidents in the factories and mills?
A: I have seen cases in which the arm has been torn off near the shoulder joint.

Photocopy original © Amnesty International UK

ACTIVITY 5 Different medical opinions

Question Sheet

Section A: Evidence

1. Interviews can be useful historical evidence because ....

   ....

2. Interviews are not always useful historical evidence because ....

   ....

3. I think that the interviews with the doctors are useful/not useful (*circle your answer*)

   historical documents because ....

   ....

Section B: Interpretation

1. Dr .... appears to support the working conditions,

   and Dr .... appears not to support them.

2. Dr .... answers the questions in very little detail. I think this is because

   ....

3. Dr .... says that the effects of standing up all day produces deformed children.

   This condition is called ....

Section C: Understanding the facts

1. In order to check whether what the doctors were saying was true I would ....

   ....

2. Dr Whatton might be wrong because ....

   ....

3. Dr Smith might be wrong because ....

   ....

Section D: My opinion

1. My opinion on the two different versions given is that ....

   ....

   ....

2. The most exhausting work I have ever done was ....

   ....

3. I think that children should/should not (*circle your answer*) be allowed to work full-time in factories

   because ....

   ....

Photocopy original © Amnesty International UK

Teachers' notes

ACTIVITY 6 Voices from Victorian factories

Aim:
To construct rules from the perspectives of different actors, using historical evidence.

Time:
40 minutes

Materials:
One copy of each Quotation Sheet for each group of four (pages 32 and 33)

What to do:
- Hand out the Quotation Sheets to each group.
- Ask each student to read out a quotation from each sheet to their group.
- Check that the class has understood the quotations.
- Students write down what they think they would be doing on an average working day between 5am and 10pm if they were a Victorian factory child with the help of evidence from the factory children quotations.
- Divide the class into two halves. Half of the group are to be employers, the other half are to be factory children and other workers. Each group must draw up a list of rules and responsibilities for the factory, to include: pay and conditions, health and safety, hours of work, time off, food, home breaks. Will there be punishments for anyone caught breaking the rules?
- Discuss results and opinions.

ACTIVITY

Photocopy original © Amnesty International UK

ACTIVITY

ACTIVITY 6 Voices from Victorian factories

Factory children speak out:

"Our regular time was from five in the morning till nine or ten at night; and on Saturday, till eleven, and often twelve at night, and then we were sent to clean the machinery on the Sunday."

John Birley, 1848

"No time was allowed for breakfast and no sitting for dinner and no time for tea."

John Birley, 1849

"The highest wages I ever had in the factory were 5s 6d. per week."

Benjamin Gomersal, 1842

"I worked from five in the morning until nine at night. I lived two miles from the mill."

Elizabeth Bentley, 1809, working from age 6

"In the morning I could scarcely walk, and my brother and sister used, out of kindness, to take me under each arm, and run with me to the mill, and my legs dragged on the ground; in consequence of the pain I could not walk."

Joseph Hebergram, 1832

"I was strapped most severely till I could not bear to sit on a chair without pillows."

Samuel Downe, 1832

"My mother is dead; my father was obliged to send me to the mill, in order to keep me."

Benjamin Gomersal, 1842

"(Mary) knocked her food can down on the floor. The Master, Mr Newton, kicked her where he should not do, and it caused her to wear away until she died."

Sarah Carpenter, 1849

Photocopy original © Amnesty International UK

ACTIVITY 6 Voices from Victorian factories

Victorian employers speak out:

"...after having rescued a great number of children from vice and misery, (we) have at a heavy expense trained them up in the habits of industry and religion, and rendered them ... some of [society's] most useful members." (1.)

"Education is what all humane masters would wish to see accomplished, but to take an hour or two from the twelve working hours would amount to surrender of all the profits..." (1.)

"Free labourers cannot be obtained to perform night work for low pay ... night work has been proved not to be injurious to the health of apprentices. So why do we need to have any new laws?" (1.)

"The apprentices, especially those from London, come from low and vicious surroundings, and need very strict discipline to reform them ..." (1.)

"The masters, harassed and tired out by the incessant complaints of their apprentices ... will be obliged to give up their works; (they) may perhaps become bankrupts or .... remove to a foreign country, leaving their apprentices a grievous load upon the parish...." (1.)

"A person constantly under the eye of his master for twelve hours together and not permitted to go out at night cannot commit crimes." (2.)

(1.) Observations on the Factory Act by Burley mill owners, 1802
(2.)Theodore Price, in evidence to Robert Peel's Committee on State of Children in Manufactories, 1816

Photocopy original © Amnesty International UK

ACTIVITY

Teachers' notes

ACTIVITY 7 Paid child labour in the UK

Aim:
This summary of paid child labour in the UK from the Industrial Revolution to the present can be used independently as support material for the Industrial Revolution, or to introduce the topic of paid child labour in general.

Time:
50-70 minutes

Materials:
- A copy of Information Sheets 1 (pages 35 and 36) and 2 (page 37) for each student.

What to do:
- Ask students to read through Information Sheet 1, presenting both sides of the argument. Point out that although all paid work can be classified as child labour, many children work sensible hours without exploitation and benefit from the experience. However, others, in the UK and overseas, are exploited. Ask the class if they were aware of the UK laws.

Discussion:
- Examine the summarised extract from the Children and Young Persons Act (1933) in Information Sheet 2. Is it reasonable? Why/why not?
- What are the main differences between the paid child labour of the Industrial Revolution and paid child labour in the UK today? Are they very different?
- Make a list of paid jobs that the students think are acceptable for children under school-leaving age to do, and a list of those which are unacceptable.

Follow-up:
- Ask students to write down all the arguments they can think of to support a minimum wage for under-18s. They can feed back to the rest of the class.
- Ask students to write down their opinions on students working under school-leaving age. They can feed back to the rest of the class.

Homework:
- Ask students to conduct a survey of as many school age students or young people as they can to find out who has a job. Include their age, and how many hours they work. The survey should be anonymous. What proportion of students who are still at school have a job? Pool the results on a class chart
- Ask each student to interview five adults (friends/family/neighbours) of different ages and record their results. They should seek answers to these questions:

i) In what year did you have your first job? How old were you?
ii) How many hours a week did you work?
iii) What kind of work did you do?

- Students then answer the following questions:

i) Does your evidence show that people started work at an older or younger age in the past compared with present times?
ii) How could you confirm the accuracy of your findings?

Photocopy original © Amnesty International UK

ACTIVITY 7 Paid child labour in the UK

Information Sheet 1

© Anti-Slavery International

Boy street vendor, UK, 1996

UK 1996 juvenile employment

Today, many school children in the UK do an early morning paper round, or have a Saturday job. It's something we take for granted, and laws govern the type of work that is safe for children, as well as hours and conditions to protect them from exploitation. Children have always worked, but there have not always been laws to protect them.

We often think child labour started with the Industrial Revolution, but it has existed since time immemorial. It was taken for granted that children would work, and help to support the

Photocopy original © Amnesty International UK

ACTIVITY 7: Information Sheet 1 (continued)

family. The main change at the time of the Industrial Revolution was in the type of work that children were expected to do. The new factories, mills and coal mines started to recruit child workers. Conditions in these places were often dangerous and hours long. It was not unusual for children to work a 15-hour day, and for their health to be seriously damaged. Fanny Drake, a young girl working in a coal mine in Yorkshire describes the effects of her work on her health:

'I have had to stand up to the calves of my legs in water. It was bad as this a fortnight at a time ... my feet were skinned, and just as if they were scalded, for the water was bad: it had stood sometime; and I was off my work owing to it, and had a headache and bleeding at my nose.'

The great period of change, both in the nature of children's work and in public attitudes, also began during the Industrial Revolution. There was an awakening of social conscience as society and government became more aware of the exploitation of the labour force. A series of Royal Commissions and government investigations looked into the problem of child labour in different sections of society. The evidence collected in these enquiries led to new laws that limited the hours that children could work, and set a minimum age for children working in dangerous industries. Towards the end of the 19th Century the Education Acts were passed, making education compulsory for all children under 10. Slowly children started to leave the workplace and spend their days at school.

Problems with child labour in the UK:

- Many children have been injured at work
- Research by the Trades Union Congress (TUC) suggests that 4 per cent of children truant from school to work
- The TUC research also shows that pay can be as little as 33p per hour
- Working long hours can affect how well a child does at school and in examinations

So why do children choose to work?

- Surveys show that many children enjoy the independence they have as a result of work
- Some children feel that they gain self-esteem at work, and respect from adults and friends
- Children enjoy the money they receive from working – especially with the pressure to have fashionable clothes, trainers, etc.
- Some children (rarely in the UK) actually need to work to earn income for their family

Fact: In the late 1990s the Low Pay Unit estimated that there were 2 million working children in the UK, and that three-quarters of these were working illegally.

Photocopy original © Amnesty International UK

ACTIVITY 7 Paid child labour in the UK

Information Sheet 2

What does the law have to say?

The International Convention on the Rights of the Child 1989 obliges states to pass laws to protect children and young persons, ensuring that they:

- do not work excessive hours
- have safe employment conditions
- do not work when they are too young to do so
- do not do work which interferes with their education.

In the United Kingdom this protection is provided through the Children and Young Persons Act 1933, updated in 1998. The law now says that young people of school age are not allowed to work:

- if they are under the age of 14 (except for some jobs such as paper rounds which are allowed from age 13)
- before 7am or after 7pm
- during school hours
- for more than two hours on a school weekday
- for more than one hour before school starts
- for more than two hours on a Sunday
- for more than eight hours (or if under 15, five hours) on Saturdays or holidays
- for more than 35 hours (or if under 15, 25 hours) a week during holidays.

The Act also says that young people are only allowed to do work which is not going to damage their health, safety or development. For example no one under 16 should operate dangerous machinery, including kitchen machinery.

The National Minimum Wage was introduced in 1999 in the UK. However, it only protects employees over 18. It remains up to employers to decide how much to pay a worker/employee aged under 18.

Source: Additional material by Alison Gurden and Rose McCausland.

ACTIVITY

Photocopy original © Amnesty International UK

ACTIVITY

Teachers' notes

The struggle for women's rights

ACTIVITY 8 Suffragettes

Aims:
This activity encourages the class to consider the activities of the suffragettes and those who opposed them in the context of human rights. Even though neither the UDHR nor the Convention on the Elimination of All Forms of Discrimination Against Women (CEDAW) were in place at the time, the suffragettes did feel that their struggle was for rights.

Time:
40 minutes plus homework

Materials:
- Two copies of the suffragettes Case Study Sheets for each pair of students, plus an overhead transparency if possible (pages 39 and 40)
- One copy of the anti-suffragette poster (page 41) for each pair of students

What to do:
- Give a Case Study Sheet to each pair and ask them to read them. Ask two students to read out their sheet in turn. These can be projected for the class to follow, or photocopies can be used. Follow this up with questions to the class. For example: *Where did the woman have her baby? Why? What is a hunger strike? What human rights were the force-feeders violating?*
- Using the poster, read through the arguments put up against the suffragettes. Comment on each.

Either:
Ask the students to design a campaign poster for the suffragettes or to write a suffragette campaign speech. This can be accompanied by relevant artwork. **Finish for homework.**

Or:
In groups of six, write the different sides of the argument as a five-minute role-play. There should be an even mix of suffragettes and those against them. It should present the different sides of the story.

Photocopy original © Amnesty International UK

ACTIVITY 8 Suffragettes

Case Study Sheet 1

Emmeline Pankhurst (speech delivered to the court, 21 October 1908)

'We have taken this action, because as women... we realise that the condition of our sex is so deplorable that it is our duty even to break the law in order to call attention to the reasons why we do so.

Now, we have tried every way. We have presented larger petitions than were ever presented for any other reform. We have faced hostile mobs at street corners because we were told that we could not have that representation for our taxes which men have won unless we converted the whole of the country to our side. Because we have done this we have been misrepresented, we have been ridiculed, we have had contempt poured upon us. The ignorant mob at the street corner have been incited to offer us violence which we have faced unarmed... We know that we need the protection of the vote even more than men have needed it.

Although the Government admitted that we are political offenders... we shall be treated as pickpockets and drunkards, we shall be searched. I want you, if you can, as a man, to realise what it means to women like us... it is our duty to make this world a better place for women than it is today.

© Mary Evans Picture Library – unattributed engraving

I was in the hospital at Holloway [prison], and when I was there I heard from one of the beds near me the moans of a woman who was in the pangs of childbirth. I should like you to realise how women feel at helpless little infants breathing their first breath in the atmosphere of a prison. We believe that if we get the vote we will find some more humane way of dealing with women like that...

We believe that if we get the vote it will mean better conditions for our unfortunate sisters. We know what the condition of a woman worker is... There are women who have been driven to live an immoral life because they cannot earn enough to live decently... We are not here because we are law-breakers, we are here in our efforts to become law-makers.'

Source: Midge Mackenzie (1975) Shoulder to Shoulder, Penguin Books

Photocopy original © Amnesty International UK

ACTIVITY 8 Suffragettes

Case Study Sheet 2

Mary Leigh (speech delivered to her solicitor, 22 September 1909)

‘On my arrival at Winston Green Gaol on Wednesday afternoon, September 22, I protested against the treatment to which I was subjected and broke the windows in my cell. Accordingly at nine o'clock in the evening I was taken to the punishment cell, a cold dark room on the ground floor. I was then stripped and handcuffed with the hands behind during the day, except at meals... On Thursday food was brought into the cell – potatoes, bread, and gruel – but I did not touch it.

About noon on Saturday I was told the matron wished to speak to me, and was taken to the doctor's room... The doctor said I was to sit down, and I did. He then said... "*you are not to be released, even on medical grounds. If you still refrain from food I must take other measures to compel you to take it...*" I then said: "*I refuse, and if you force food on me, I want to know how you are going to do it.*" He said: "*That is a matter for me to decide...*" I was then surrounded and forced back on to the chair, which was tilted backward. There were about 10 persons around me. The doctor then forced my mouth so as to form a pouch, and held me while one of the wardresses poured some liquid from a spoon; it was milk and brandy... On Saturday afternoon the wardresses forced me on to the bed and the two doctors came in with them. While I was held down a nasal tube was inserted. It is two yards long with a funnel at the end; there is a glass junction in the middle to see if the liquid is passing. The end is put up the right and left nostril on alternate days. Great pain is experienced during the process, both mental and physical.

The sensation is most painful – the drums of the ears seem to be bursting. There is a horrible pain in the throat and the breast. The tube is pushed down 20 inches... The one holding the funnel end pours the liquid down about a pint of milk, or egg and milk sometimes... The after-effects are a feeling of faintness, a sense of great pain in the diaphragm or breastbone, in the nose and ears. The tube must go down below the breastbone, though I cannot feel it there.

I was very sick on the first occasion after the tube was withdrawn. I have also suffered from bad indigestion... I have used no violence, though having provocation in being fed by force. I resist and am overcome by weight of numbers. If the doctor does not think the fluid is going down sufficiently swiftly he pinches my nose with the tube in it, and my throat causing me increased pain.’

Source: Midge Mackenzie (1975) Shoulder to Shoulder, Penguin Books

© The Fawcett Library

Photocopy original © Amnesty International UK

ACTIVITY 8 Suffragettes

© Montage by Dan Jones Amnesty International UK

Photocopy original © Amnesty International UK

ACTIVITY

Teachers' notes

ACTIVITY 9 Rights of women timeline

Aim:
This timeline activity is one way to help students to think about the continuity of the women's rights movement rather than boxing it into a particular period. This timeline activity shows that the struggle of the suffragettes was not an isolated event. They 'stood on giants' shoulders' and others followed.

Time:
40 minutes

Materials:
- A set of Timeline Cards (page 44) for each group, copied on to card, and cut so the information and the dates are separated
- One copy of the Information Sheet on the suffragettes (page 43)
- One overhead transparency of the Timeline Cards (page 44)
- One copy of CEDAW (pages 72 and 73)

What to do:
- Read the Information Sheet out to the class, stopping to emphasise the dates and explain the key phrases.
- Give one set of cards to each small group and ask them to match the events and dates. There is a blank card for 2000+. What might be put in the blank space? Encourage them to think of rights issues – for example, health, education, relationships, law, etc.
- Now put up the transparency. Give groups a chance to look to compare. How successful were they in matching up? Which were easiest? You may want to read extracts from the Information Sheet again and encourage the students to indicate when they hear the details from the cards being read aloud. Are there responsibilities that go with these rights?
- For those who are interested, the copy of CEDAW on pages 72 and 73 can be shown.

Photocopy original © Amnesty International UK

ACTIVITY 9 Rights of women timeline

Information Sheet

The struggle for women's rights

The suffragettes fought for womens suffrage, the right for women to vote in parliamentary elections, by militant, non-violent means.

Other groups, men as well as women, worked for women's suffrage by lobbying, demonstrations, pressing for bills in Parliament and educating women and the public. The constitutional suffragists, led by Millicent Fawcett, worked from the 1860s, obtaining bills in 37 out of 44 years between 1870 and 1914, but those which were passed in the House of Commons were defeated in the Lords.

From the 1890s, women working in the cotton trades in Lancashire and Cheshire, the radical suffragists, organised meetings and demonstrations and worked for parliamentary candidates and MPs who supported women's suffrage.

From 1906, the Women's Labour League campaigned for women's suffrage and encouraged women to stand for election to local authorities to work for better food and health services for poor women and their children.

From 1900 to 1914, many groups and organisations were formed to work for women's right to vote in parliamentary elections. They included the Women's Freedom League, the Actresses' Franchise League and the Northern Men's Federation for Women's Suffrage.

The demand for women's rights went back more than 200 years. It included demands for a good education for girls and women so they could earn a living; access to jobs and professions; mothers to have custody of their children when separated or divorced; married women to own and control their own property; the right to be recognised as full citizen; the right to vote in all elections and to be eligible for elected or appointed office on the same terms as men. Many demands of the 'First Women's Movement' were won only after World War I.

Among the 19th Century activists for women's rights were Dorothea Beale, Frances Mary Buss and Emily Davies for education, Elizabeth Garrett Anderson (sister of Millicent Fawcett) and Sophia Jex-Blake for medicine, Josephine Butler for the protection of women in relation to prostitution and against the Contagious Diseases Acts.

In the second half of the 20th Century, women found that the rights they had won were merely the removal of disqualifications. The 'Second Women's Movement', Women's Liberation, from the end of the 1960s, demanded the end of discrimination; equal pay; good provision for child care; women's control of their own bodies (contraception and abortion); and action against violence against women.

The Abortion Act of 1967, despite difficulties in availability and repeated attempts to make it ineffective, has largely ended backstreet abortions. The Equal Pay Act 1970, the Sex Discrimination Act 1975 and European Directives have increased women's access to a wide range of careers and occupations, though much remains to be achieved. Domestic violence, rape and violence against women have been on the political agenda since the 1970s.

But women are still discriminated against. Pay is still far from equal although pay rates may appear the same, violence against women is not adequately dealt with and only a beginning has been made in providing adequate childcare.

Source: Dr Margherita Rendel

ACTIVITY

Photocopy original © Amnesty International UK

ACTIVITY 9 Rights of women timeline

Timeline Cards

Cut here!

1860s	Millicent Fawcett campaigned to have bills passed in Parliament to achieve women's suffrage
1890s	Women working in the cotton trades in Lancashire and Cheshire organised meetings and demonstrations for women's rights
from 1906	The Women's Labour League campaigned for women's suffrage and encouraged women to stand for election to local authorities
1900-1914	Many groups and organisations were formed in support of women's suffrage
1918	The Representation of the People Act gave the vote to women over 30 with a property qualification, or who were graduates
1928	Full women's suffrage
1960s	When it became clear that the rights gained were mainly the removal of disqualifications, the second women's movement, Women's Liberation, was formed. It demanded an end to discrimination, equal pay, good child-care provision, access to contraception/abortion, and action to stop violence against women
1967	The Abortion Act
1970	The Equal Pay Act
1975	The Sex Discrimination Act Directives of the European Union on equal pay, non-discrimination at work and pensions
1979	UN Convention on the Elimination of All Forms of Discrimination Against Women (CEDAW)
1990s	Directives of the European Union on parental leave and trade union rights at work
2002+	

Photocopy original © Amnesty International UK

Teachers' notes

ACTIVITY 10 Women fighting for human rights

Aim:
To undertake research via the Internet either as homework or in the classroom. If you do not have access to the Internet, the same activities can be followed if sufficient copies of textbooks or encyclopaedias are available.

This activity focuses on **Elizabeth Garrett Anderson** and **Marie Stopes** as examples of women who made an impact on the way women experience life today. You may choose to research some of the many other pioneers of women's rights in this country, for example: Annie Besant, Frances Buss, Josephine Butler, Emily Davison, Mary Macarthur, Susan Lawrence, Eleanor Marx, Beatrice Webb, Ellen Wilkinson, and Mary Wollstonecraft.

Time:
40-45 minutes

Materials:
- One copy of the Research Sheet for each computer (page 46)
- If you are not doing this lesson on the Internet, check that you have sufficient classroom resources

What to do:
Ask students to:
- Sign on to the website of **Spartacus Educational http://www.spartacus.schoolnet.co.uk**
- Enter the pages called **Encyclopedia of British History 1700-1900.**
- Scroll down until they see the heading **Emancipation of Women** and click on it.
- Scroll down until they find the names of Elizabeth Garrett Anderson and Marie Stopes and click on one of them.
- Each group (or individual) works through the Research Sheet on page 46, finding the answers from the website as well as their own reflections.
- If using resources other than the Internet, students complete the activity sheets using the resources available.

Homework:
Ask students to research at least one other woman in history who has campaigned on behalf of other people. It does not necessarily have to be for and on the behalf of women only. They can write down her achievements either in essay style, as a report, or in a grid.

Follow-up:
Once the work on Anderson and Stopes is complete the students can move on to write their obituary. This could be explained at the start of the lesson. Obituaries can be put on display and/or graded. Students who finish their grid quickly can research the second of the two women.

Source: The Spartacus Educational Website – http://www.spartacus.schoolnet.co.uk operational March 2002

ACTIVITY

Photocopy original © Amnesty International UK

ACTIVITY

ACTIVITY 10 Women fighting for human rights

Research Sheet

Read the questions carefully before answering them. If you are working in a group and you have different opinions it is fine to write them all down.

Research questions	Answers
1. Between which years was she alive?	
2. Family background (eg parents, husband, occupation, children etc)	
3. Campaigned for the ...	i) ii) iii)
4. Anything else?	
5. What did she achieve?	i) ii) iii)
6. Anything else?	

Follow-up:

Once this sheet is complete, show it to your teacher and ask for permission to start the obituary.

Using a complete side/sheet of paper write the obituary (memorial statement) for your chosen historical figure. It should mention her name, dates, and achievements among other things. You can illustrate this with relevant pictures.

Photocopy original © Amnesty International UK

Teachers' notes

The Holocaust

ACTIVITY 11 The Holocaust and human rights

Aim:

To introduce students to the articles in the Universal Declaration of Human Rights (UDHR) with reference to the Holocaust. The situations which students are asked to consider are actual historical events. The activity can be used to introduce the Holocaust or to reinforce previous lessons on it.

After matching up the situation cards to the numbered articles in the UDHR, the students will have considered several human rights issues and will have read through the UDHR.

Time:

40 minutes

Materials:

- One set of Situation Cards (page 48 and 49) per group, each set in a different envelope, or a photocopy of the card sheets
- A copy of the UDHR for each group, in A3 size (pages 68 and 69)
- One copy of the UDHR Grid (page 50) for each group.

What to do:

- Give each group one set of situation cards, a copy of the UDHR, and the grid.
- Explain that the events described took place in Germany and Nazi-occupied Europe.
- The groups read the situation cards and look at the UDHR to see which articles are being infringed. In some situations there may be many violations. Write the numbers of the articles that are being violated in the appropriate box on the grid.

Discussion:

Ask each group in turn to read out the numbers of the articles they have written in the box. Do other groups agree? Any more to add? Can they justify this?

Do the students have questions about the stories and the UDHR? Encourage them to reflect on the similarities and differences between group findings.

ACTIVITY

Photocopy original © Amnesty International UK

ACTIVITY

ACTIVITY 11 The Holocaust and human rights

Situation Cards 1

A.
Plaszow labour camp forced 20,000 Jews to work without pay. More than 9,000 workers died from exhaustion. In concentration camps across Europe men, women and children lived in dormitories in appalling conditions.

B.
In October 1939, all Roma Roma ('gypsies') were ordered to be sent to concentration camps.

C.
On 16 November 1938, all state schools were closed to Jewish children.

D.
80,000-100,000 disabled children and adults were victims of Nazi mass murder.

E.
Jewish people were not allowed to visit cafés, pools or parks where there were non-Jews.

F.
From early 1933, Hitler and his government ended constitutional rights, created a one-party totalitarian state and imposed their ideology on Germany and all the areas they subsequently controlled.

G.
Almost all the synagogues (Jewish places of worship) were deliberately destroyed by the Nazis during the Second World War.

H.
In December 1938, all Jewish publishing houses and bookshops were told that they were to be closed down by the end of the year.

I.
The Nazis made homosexuality illegal. The death penalty for all homosexual people found in the SS and police was introduced in 1943.

Photocopy original © Amnesty International UK

ACTIVITY 11 The Holocaust and human rights

Situation Cards 2

J. Many Jews fled from Nazi territories to other countries. Some were refused admittance.	**K.** The Nuremberg Laws, passed on 15 September 1935, barred Jewish people from being German citizens and took away some of their most basic rights. For example, marriages between Jews and other Germans were forbidden.	**L.** Many governments and organisations are still in possession of property and money which belonged to the Jews.
M. Towards the end of the war in 1945, some children and adults were rescued from concentration camps. Most others had died from starvation, illness, overwork, gassing and execution.	**N.** In many of the concentration camps, 'medical experiments', in fact torture, took place. An example of this was injecting blue dye into the eyes of brown-eyed people to make them 'Aryan-blue'.	

ACTIVITY

Photocopy original © Amnesty International UK

ACTIVITY

ACTIVITY 11 The Holocaust and human rights

The Universal Declaration of Human Rights Grid

Read the situations and find out which articles of the UDHR are being abused. There may be more than one article being abused in one situation. Write the numbers of the articles in the appropriate box.

A:	**B:**	**C:**	**D:**
E:	**F:**	**G:**	**H:**
I:	**J:**	**K:**	**L:**
M:	**N:**		

Photocopy original © Amnesty International UK

Teachers' notes

ACTIVITY 12 Anne Frank

Aims:
To enable students to learn about the experiences of Anne Frank and her family during the Holocaust through the website and from Anne's diary. Students are asked to make the link between the Holocaust and racism today and think about how we can prevent such abuses of basic human rights. The activity sheet is differentiated by outcome although some students may need help when they are working with the website. If you are not in a position to use the Internet you can use the photocopiable version of the website information given on pages 52 and 53.

Time:
40 minutes plus homework and follow-up

Materials:
- Access to the web (or use the paper version of the Anne Frank website given on pages 52 and 53 as Information Sheet 1).
- One copy of Activity Sheets 1 and 2 (pages 54 and 55) for each computer.

What to do:
- Ask students to log on to the website of the **Anne Frank Centre USA** www.annefrank.com, or read the Information Sheets.
- Each group (or individual) at a computer works through the Activity Sheets, using the website as well as their own ideas to answer.

Homework:
- Ask the students to think about how it feels to be discriminated against. This still happens today, in the UK and elsewhere in the world. Ask them to write diary extracts describing what is being said or done, and how they feel about it.
- Ask students to design their own website, on paper, for school students who might be suffering from abuse. They should give practical advice about what to do and who might be able to help. Remind students that websites are usually made up of words and art. They can look at other websites to give them ideas.

Follow-up:
- Students can develop a class display on the link between the discrimination of the Holocaust and discrimination today.
- Develop Internet lessons using the following sites: The Anne Frank Educational Trust UK **www.afet.org.uk**
Anne Frank Timeline **www.uen.org**
- Using a copy of the UDHR (pages 68-69) and CERD (pages 74-75), students can identify which basic rights were infringed during the Holocaust. The same activity can be done using examples of recent racism in the news.
- Students can read the *Diary of Anne Frank* in full.

Source: The Anne Frank Centre USA Website — http:www.annefrank.com
Huntington School History Department, York, UK.
Email: pc.mountford@huntington-ed.org.uk

ACTIVITY

Photocopy original © Amnesty International UK

ACTIVITY 12 Anne Frank

Information Sheet 1: Anne's story

These sheets are to use as an alternative to going directly to the Anne Frank website.

Anne Frank, born on 12 June 1929, was the second daughter of Otto and Edith Frank, both from respected German-Jewish families. Otto could trace his family heritage in Frankfurt back to the 17th Century. Anne and her older sister Margot were brought up in Germany in an atmosphere of tolerance; the Franks had friends of many faiths and nationalities.

However, things altered dramatically for the Frank family. In the summer of 1933, Otto Frank left Frankfurt for Amsterdam to set up a branch of his brother's company, the Dutch Opekta Company. Less than a year later, Edith, Margot and Anne (then four years old) joined Otto. Unfortunately, the Franks' belief that Amsterdam offered them a safe haven from Nazism was shattered when, in May 1940, Germany invaded the Netherlands. The Franks were again forced to live under Nazi rule.

The Nazis started to issue anti-Jewish decrees. In May 1942 all Jews aged six or over were required to wear a yellow Star of David to set them apart from non-Jews. All Jews had to register their businesses and hand them over to non-Jews. By 1942 mass arrests of Jews and their transportation to German work camps was common. The Franks began to prepare to go into hiding, and already had a place in mind – attics above Otto Frank's office (referred to by Anne as their 'secret annexe').

© AFF/AFS.Amsterdam

Mr Frank also made arrangements for his business partners (the Pfeffers) and their son Peter to share the hideaway. Meanwhile Anne's sister Margot received a call-up notice to be deported to a Nazi 'work camp'. The Frank family realised that they would have to move right away. They hurriedly packed their belongings and left notes implying that they had left the country. With the Franks, the van Pelks and another resident, Fritz Pfeffer, there were eight people in the annexe. For two years they all lived there, sharing a confined space and living in constant dread of detection and arrest by the Nazis. The families were helped and supported by the Dutch employees of Mr Frank who provided food and other necessities during the time the families were in hiding. They risked their lives to do so.

The people in hiding were arrested, and on 8 August 1944, after a brief stay in prison, the residents of the annexe were moved to Westerbork transit camp until 3 September, when they were transported to the Auschwitz death camp in Poland. Anne and Margot contracted typhus and grew very sick. Anne, 15 years old, and Margot, 19 years old, died in February and March 1945.

Word list

family heritage: the history of your family, its traditions and belongings
tolerance: allowing people to live together peacefully and with acceptance of one another
National Socialist Party: the political party led by Adolf Hitler which discriminated against many people, in particular Jewish people, black people, Roma ('gypsies'), disabled people, gay people and women
decrees: official laws; people were punished for failing to abide by them
annexe: a small space within or attached to a building

Photocopy original © Amnesty International UK

ACTIVITY 12 Anne Frank

Information Sheet 2: Anne's diary

On 12 June 1942, Anne Frank's parents gave her a small red and white plaid diary for her 13th birthday. Anne recorded her innermost feelings in her diary, which she named 'Kitty'. Less that a month after receiving her diary, on 6 July 1942, Anne and her family were forced to go into hiding. Though they could take very few things with them to their hiding place, Anne took her diary. During the months Anne lived in hiding, her diary became her best friend and confidant.

These extracts come with kind permission from the Anne Frank Centre USA's website: www.annefrank.com
Their email address is afc@annefrank.com

'Our many Jewish friends and acquaintances are being taken away in droves. The Gestapo is treating them very roughly and transporting them in cattle cars to Westerbork, the big camp in Drenthe to which they're sending all the Jews ... If it's that bad in Holland, what must it be like in those faraway and uncivilised places where the Germans are sending them? We assume that most of them are being murdered. The English radio says they're being gassed.'

9 October, 1942

'Have you ever head of the term "hostages"? That's the latest punishment for saboteurs. It's the most horrible thing you can imagine. Leading citizens – innocent people – are taken prisoner to await their execution. If the Gestapo can't find the saboteur, they simply grab five hostages and line them up against the wall. You read the announcements of their death in the paper, where they're referred to as "fatal accidents".'

9 October, 1942

'Fine specimens of humanity, those Germans, and to think I'm actually one of them! No, that's not true, Hitler took away our nationality long ago, and besides, there are no greater enemies on earth than the Germans and Jews.'

9 October, 1942

'I've reached a point where I hardly care whether I live or die. The world will keep on turning without me, and I can't do anything to change events anyway. I'll just let matters take their course and concentrate on studying and hope that everything will be all right in the end.'

3 February, 1944

Photocopy original © Amnesty International UK

ACTIVITY

ACTIVITY 12 Anne Frank

Activity Sheet 1

• Have in front of you a copy of extracts from the Anne Frank Centre USA, or visit their website: www.annefrank.com

• First browse through the site or pages from the site

• Now read the questions carefully before answering them

Anne's story

1. When was Anne Frank born?

2. What do you think is significant about the fact that Otto Frank could trace his family heritage back to the 17th Century?

3. Explain the meaning of 'Anne and her older sister were brought up in Germany in an atmosphere of tolerance'.

4. Why do you think the Franks left Germany in the 1930s?

5. Why do you think the Jews were made to wear the Star of David?

6. How do you think you would feel if you had to wear the Star of David? Circle the words.

embarrassed	noticeable
proud	humiliated
religious	frightened
in danger	safer

Anything else?

7. Write a few sentences to describe what you think it must have been like living in the annexe.

8. Anne and Margot were taken to Auschwitz in September 1944, where they eventually died. What was it like to be there?

Photocopy original © Amnesty International UK

ACTIVITY 12 Anne Frank

Activity Sheet 2

Anne's diary

1. What did Anne call her diary?

2. Why do you think Anne's diary has sold over 24 million copies in over 55 different languages?

3. In her diary Anne often refers to 'the Germans' as being the ones who were persecuting the Jews. Do you think that all of the Germans were? If not, who is she really writing about?

4. What do you think Anne means in the diary entry where she says that 'Hitler took away our nationality long ago'?

After the Holocaust

1. There are some people today who will not forgive what the Nazis did to the Jews (as well as many other targeted groups). What is your opinion on this?

2. Write down any other situations that you have heard of in the news, where discrimination against whole groups of people is still continuing.

3. The Universal Declaration of Human Rights was written after the Holocaust to make sure that nothing like it ever happened again. But the human rights of many people are still abused for who they are and what they represent. What should be done to stop this?

Photocopy original © Amnesty International UK

ACTIVITY

Teachers' notes

ACTIVITY 13 Those who struggled for our rights

Aims:
Throughout history, individuals and groups have struggled to achieve justice for themselves and others. Today we might call them human rights defenders. This activity introduces the CVs of seven such people.

Time:
40 minutes

Materials:
- Paper
- Access to library or the Internet
- Tape recorder
- One copy of the introductory autobiography on a human rights defender for each group (pages 57 to 63).

What to do
- Divide the class into seven groups.
- Hand each group the introductory autobiography on their human rights defender:

  Bartolomé de las Casas
  Sojourner Truth
  Jean Henri Dunant
  Mahatma Gandhi
  Eglantyne Jebb
  Eleanor Roosevelt
  Peter Benenson
- Each group of students should find out more information about their human rights defender using the web or the library.
- They should imagine that their human rights defender comes to visit the school and gives a talk to a school assembly about their cause. One person in each group takes on the role of the human rights defender, choosing an appropriate moment in their career for their visit. Other members of the group take on the role of journalists on the local newspaper or radio station. They have to prepare an article for the newspaper or make a tape for a radio or TV broadcast about the human rights defender's visit to their school. This will include an interview with the human rights defender. Some reports should be written in a way that is sympathetic to the aims and activity of the human rights defender. Other reports should be written in a way that is critical of what the defender stands for or has done.
- Where possible students should base their statements on historical evidence, with facts and using the actual words used at the time. However, they must use their imagination to describe what was said and what happened at the meeting. 'Vox pop' audience reactions could also be sought from school students and from members of the public.

Source: Dan Jones, Amnesty International

Photocopy original © Amnesty International UK

ACTIVITY 13 Those who struggled for our rights

ACTIVITY

Bartolomé de las Casas
1474?-1566

© Mary Evans Picture Library – unattributed engraving

1474?	I was born in Seville. My father was a merchant adventurer who sailed with Columbus.
1493	I fought against the Moors in Granada. I studied Latin and theology at the Academy of Seville Cathedral.
1498	I passed my law degree at Salamanca University and became a religious teacher.
1502	I sailed on Columbus's third expedition to the Indies with the new governor of Hispaniola. I preached among the Indian peoples.
1506	I became a deacon in Rome.
1511	I heard a Christmas sermon by Antonio de Montesinos, a Dominican priest who spoke out against the cruel treatment of Indians. I gave up my *encomienda* of Indian slaves, and began to campaign against Indian enslavement.
1513	I witnessed the bloody Spanish expedition to Cuba. I tried to stop the cruelty to the Indians.
1516	I returned to Spain to plead the Indians' cause at court and in the Church.
1520/3	The Spanish regent appointed me 'Protector of the Indies'. I tried (unsuccessfully) to build a utopian community in Venezuela where Spanish and Indian people could live together in harmony.
1523	I became Dominican friar in Santo Domingo, where I wrote the history of the Spanish conquest of 'New Spain'. I also worked in Peru, Guatemala, Mexico and Nicaragua.
1537	Pope Paul III said that Indians were human and to be treated with respect.
1542	I met the Spanish King Charles V and got new laws passed limiting the *encomienda* system and slavery. I published some books and my pamphlet about the abuse of the Indians, *A very brief Account of the Destruction of the Indies*, which caused a great scandal.
1543	I became Bishop of Chiapas in Guatemala. I was hated by the settlers, but respected by the Indians.
1547	I returned to Spain to lobby officials there about the human rights of the Indians.
1550	I took part in the great debate in Valladolid on slavery with Juan Sepulveda, the colonists' spokesman.

1566 *Bartolomé de las Casas died in the Convent of Santa Maria de Atocha in Spain.*

Photocopy original © Amnesty International UK

ACTIVITY 13 Those who struggled for our rights

Sojourner Truth
1797?-1883

© Hulton Getty

1797?	Round about this time, I was born as Isabella Baumfree, a slave, one of 10 children, in New York State, in the United States of America.
1806	I was sold for $100 to the Neely family in New York.
1806-1824	I had 13 children. Most of them were sold into slavery.
1824	I escaped from slavery with the help of the Quakers. I joined an abolitionist community in Massachusetts.
1826	I won a legal case and was able to rescue my youngest son from slavery. I took on my new name of 'Sojourner Truth'.
1827-80	Although I never learned to read or write, I travelled the country preaching sermons against slavery and injustice and for religious faith, for women's rights and against alcohol. Often I spoke to white audiences.
1850	I dictated my autobiography to my friend, who wrote it down.
1851	I made a speech on the emancipation of slaves – 'Ain't I a Woman?' – to the Women's Rights Convention in Ohio. It became very famous.
1861-4	In the American Civil War I raised money for the black soldiers in the Union regiments and I distributed food and clothes.
1864	After the Civil War I worked with ex-slaves and I helped them find accommodation. I met President Lincoln and I helped to integrate the Washington trolley buses.
1864-83	I travelled around the country campaigning for the emancipation of women.

1883 *Sojourner Truth died in Battle Creek, Michigan.*

Photocopy original © Amnesty International UK

ACTIVITY 13 Those who struggled for our rights

Jean Henri Dunant
1828-1910

© Hulton Getty

1828	I was born in Switzerland, and grew up in a wealthy and religious Protestant home.
1849	I represented the Young Men's Christian Association (YMCA) in France, Belgium and Holland.
1854	I emigrated to Algeria, and started up in business in Setif.
1858	I wrote a pamphlet against slavery in the USA and in Muslim lands. I wanted to build a mill at Mons Gémila in Algeria but needed water rights.
1859	I went to Italy to get help with my water rights from Emperor Napoleon III. He was fighting a war to drive Austria out of Italy. I witnessed the terrible Battle of Solferino – where 40,000 were wounded or killed. I organised teams of volunteers to care for the casualties.
1862	I wrote a book – *A memoir of Solférino* – about the battle, the carnage, my experiences of caring for the wounded and the need to set up societies to care for the sick and wounded in war. I said an international body should be set up for this purpose.
1863	I started the International Red Cross Committee with five other Swiss men. I persuaded Switzerland to convene an international humanitarian aid conference.
1864	Twelve nations came to the conference. They adopted the First Geneva Convention on soldiers and civilians in war. They set up the Red Cross as a neutral voluntary aid society. Our emblem was the Swiss flag with colours reversed.
I867	My business collapsed. I owed 1 million Swiss francs. I was declared a bankrupt. My friends were ruined. I fled from Geneva and the scandal to live in exile in Paris. I worked on international treaties to get the Red Cross to also cover naval warfare and victims of natural disaster.
1867	I called for a neutral Palestine, and for an international library for world masterpieces.
1872	I appealed for international treaties for prisoners of war and for the peaceful settlement of international disputes.
1875	I organised a conference against the slave trade. During the Franco-Prussian war I introduced the first soldiers' identity discs – 'dog tags'.
1875-1910	I lived out the rest of my life in solitude and poverty in the Swiss village of Heiden.
1901	I was awarded one of the first Nobel Peace Prizes.

1910 *Henri Dunant died in Switzerland.*

Photocopy original © Amnesty International UK

ACTIVITY 13 Those who struggled for our rights

Mahatma Gandhi
1869-1948

© Hulton Getty

1869	I was born Mohandas Karamchand Gandhi in Porbandar, Gujarat, India. My father was adviser to a local ruler.
1883	I married my beloved Kasturba. I was 13, she was 12.
1888	I went to London to study law and qualified as a barrister. I read Hindu literature: *Bhagavad Gita*. I became vegetarian and pacifist.
1891	I practised law in Bombay.
1893	I sailed to South Africa to join an Indian law firm. I worked for the rights of South Africa's Asian community. I studied different religious faiths and developed the theory and practice of *satyagraha* – non-violent protest. I started the Indian National Congress of South Africa. We organised struggles against racial discrimination. I led strikes of miners and indentured labourers. Sometimes I was imprisoned.
1915	I returned to India and travelled widely, campaigning for the rights of indigo workers and weavers. I began leading the campaign for Indian independence from Britain.
1919	I developed the non-co-operation movement and passive resistance. I protested at the British Army's massacre of Sikhs at Amritsar.
1920	I started my own spinning in a campaign against British textiles and for economic self-sufficiency.
1922	I was jailed for protesting against the Rowlatt Bills. These made it illegal to oppose the British. I was to spend seven years in prison.
1924	I fasted against communal violence between Hindu and Muslim communities.
1930	I organised the 180-mile Dandi Salt protest march and a national one-day strike. Thousands were arrested.
1931	I came to London for round table talks on independence for India.
1933	I worked with the 'untouchable' *dalits*. I called them *'Harijans'* (the Children of God). I worked against the caste system.
1934	I worked in the North West Frontier.
1943	During World War II I was jailed as a member of the 'Quit India' campaign.
1945	The Muslim League called for a special homeland for Muslims – Pakistan.
1946/7	Inter-communal riots broke out in Calcutta, Delhi, Noakhali and Bihar: 1 million people died, 10 million refugees fled both ways across the borders of what were to become independent India and Pakistan. I fasted for peace.

1948	*Gandhi was shot dead by a Hindu nationalist gunman.*

Photocopy original © Amnesty International UK

ACTIVITY 13 Those who struggled for our rights

Eglantyne Jebb
1876-1928

© Save the Children

1876	I was born to a wealthy Quaker family in Ellesmere, Shropshire.
1895	I studied history at Lady Margaret Hall, Oxford University. I trained as a primary school teacher in Stockwell, London.
1899	I taught in a school in Wiltshire.
1901	I moved to Cambridge and worked with an organisation that was developing effective charity work.
1904	I made a study of poverty in Cambridge and published a report on my research.
1910	I travelled across Europe.
1913	Encouraged by my brother-in-law, Charles Buxton, I helped to organise emergency relief for refugees fleeing the war in Macedonia, in the Balkans.
1914	Although I was a pacifist and opposed the First World War, I wrote war reports for the *Cambridge Magazine*. I was respected as a journalist and translator.
1919	I was worried about the effect of the international blockade of Austria after the war. I helped to set up the Fight the Famine Council. I was arrested in Trafalgar Square and fined for handing out pictures of starving Austrian children. I launched the Save the Children Fund with my sister Dorothy in the Royal Albert Hall. It was the world's first effective international development aid organisation. We raised large sums of money through appeals and advertising
1920	I set up the International Save the Children Union of different Save the Children groups.
1921	I organised famine relief for children in the Volga region of Communist Russia.
1923	I worked on refugee relief and education in Bulgaria and Hungary. I wrote the Declaration on the Rights of the Child while walking in the Swiss mountains.
1924	My paper was adopted by the League of Nations as the International Declaration on the Rights of Child. (The United Nations Convention on the Rights of the Child, 1989, was based on it.)
1925	I helped to establish the International Child Welfare League in Geneva.
1926	Although I was ill and fragile I visited refugees in Bulgaria.
1927	I made plans for a visit to China.

1928 *Eglantyne Jebb died of a heart attack in Geneva.*

ACTIVITY

Photocopy original © Amnesty International UK

ACTIVITY

ACTIVITY 13 Those who struggled for our rights

Eleanor Roosevelt
1884-1962

© Hulton Getty

1884	I was born in New York, in the United States of America. My uncle was President Theodore Roosevelt. My childhood was not happy. My mother died of diphtheria when I was eight. My father became an alcoholic and died in a mental institution when I was 10.
1903	After a good education, I became engaged to my cousin, Franklin Delano Roosevelt. I joined the Junior League of New York, and worked in a settlement, teaching dance to immigrants.
1905	I married FDR, and worked for the Consumer League researching conditions in the clothing trade.
1905-21	I raised six children.
1921	FDR was paralysed by polio. I became his eyes and ears. I taught history at Tadhunter School; I worked as a lecturer on social problems; I was a radio broadcaster with my own show. I campaigned against child labour, and for a minimum wage and workers' protection. I joined the League of Women Voters (women had the vote by then).
1928	FDR was elected governor of New York.
1931	FDR, the Democrat candidate, was elected President.
1935	I was the First Lady but I still wrote a daily newspaper column, 'My Day', and worked for civil rights and equality.
1945	FDR, after four terms as President, died.
1946	I was chosen as the USA's delegate to the United Nations. I became chair of the UN Human Rights Commission.
1948	I helped draft the Universal Declaration of Human Rights.
1961	I was the Chair of the UN Commission on the Status of Women.

1962 *Eleanor Roosevelt died in New York.*

Photocopy original © Amnesty International UK

ACTIVITY 13 Those who struggled for our rights

Peter Benenson
1921-

© Amnesty International

1921 I was born in England into a wealthy family. My grandfather was Grigor Benenson, a Russian Jewish banker. My father was an army colonel. He died when I was young. I was brought up as a Catholic. My mother, Mrs Flora Solomon, was a very radical woman.

1932 I was educated at home for a time. One of my tutors was the writer W H Auden.

1934 I went to Eton. The Headmaster wrote to warn my mother about my 'revolutionary tendencies'.

1936 When I was 16 I organised my first international campaign. At school I raised money to care for orphan Republican children of the Spanish Civil War.

1938 I raised £4,000 with friends at school for the rescue of Jewish children from Nazi Germany and organised their adoption.

1939 I went to Oxford and read literature.

1943 I joined the army. During the war I worked in the Press Office of the Ministry of Information.

1945 I became a lawyer and was especially interested in international law.

1953 The British Trades Union Congress sent me to Spain to observe the trial of trade unionists arrested by the fascist government of General Franco.

1959 I started Justice, the British Section of the International Commission of Jurists.
I organised lawyers to observe trials in South Africa, Hungary and Cyprus.

1960 On the tube going to work I was enraged to read about two Portuguese students jailed for seven years for drinking a toast to freedom. I decided to start a new organisation to fight for human rights.

1961 In May *The Observer* and other newspapers published 'The Forgotten Prisoners', my appeal for an international campaign to release the world's prisoners of conscience and stop torture. Many volunteers joined. I set up a little office for the new organisation in my chambers.

1962 I called the new human rights organisation 'Amnesty International'. Its symbol is a candle wrapped in barbed wire. Its motto is: 'It is better to light one candle than to curse the darkness.' Sections of Amnesty began to be organised in many countries. Missions were sent to seven states and 200 case files were opened.

1977 Amnesty International was awarded the Nobel Peace Prize for its work for prisoners of conscience, for fair political trials, for an end to torture and executions.

1980 I started a society for people like me who suffer from coeliac disease.

1981 I became Chair of a new organisation called Christians Against Torture.

2001 On its 40th birthday the organisation that I started had a million members in 150 countries – the biggest human rights movement in the world.

Photocopy original © Amnesty International UK

ACTIVITY

Teachers' notes

ACTIVITY 14 Human rights history quiz

Aim:
To enable students to test and recap what they have learned.

Time:
40 minutes

Materials:
• Select the parts of the quiz covering areas that the students have studied and photocopy them (page 65).

What to do:
Give out the question sheets. Students can fill in answers individually, or in groups, or it can be organised into a round robin with everyone answering one question and then passing the sheet on.

When they have finished they can swap their answers for marking. Ask what answers people have come up with. In some cases there may be a whole range of right answers that can be discussed. The Answers sheet (page 66) can be handed out after the discussion.

Photocopy original © Amnesty International UK

ACTIVITY 14 Human rights history quiz

Slavery and child workers

1. What every slave would like to be ....
2. Anti-Slavery In..........................al campaigns for the end of all slavery.
3. To release someone from slavery is to them. ....
4. Why were some children in the 1800s called factory children? ....
5. True or false? – Many countries still allow children to work in factories instead of attending school...
6. ..Many children around the world are forced to work because their families are living in ....
7. Name an international convention, which prohibits child slavery. ....

The Holocaust and conflict

1. ....The mass murder of Jews by the Nazis in World War II is known as the ....
2. It is estimated that .... million Jews were murdered in World War II.
3. Whose diary, written during World War II, is a true story of a teenage girl persecuted because she was Jewish? ....
4. ....Identify three rights that may be violated during a conflict.. ....
5. During conflict innocent people ....
6. A.................... bombs were dropped in Hiroshima and Nagasaki.
7. People forced to leave their countries during conflicts, become known as r...........................

Equal rights

1. Emmeline Pankhurst campaigned for women to have the right to vote. She was a ....
2. ....What does CEDAW stand for? (hint: it is an international convention to protect women's rights).................................. ....
3. The system which prevented black people in South Africa having the same rights as white people was known as A ....
4. What is the name of the first black president of South Africa? ....
5. To treat one group less fairly than others is to d...
6. Give three reasons why all people should have equal rights ....
7. True or false? 'Disabled people give nothing to society and do not need equal rights' ....

International organisations

1. What international organisation has most member states? ....
2. The U................... D........................... of H.................. R.................. promotes equal rights for all.
3. Which international convention deals with the rights of children and young people? ....
4. The European C.. on Human Rights was adopted in 1951.
5. International w............. c............................ tribunals are judging allegations of genocide (mass killing of an ethnic group) in the former Yugoslavia and Rwanda.
6. Who is the current United Nations Commissioner for Human Rights? ....
7. Name five rights which you use every day that appear in international human rights conventions. ....

Photocopy original © Amnesty International UK

ACTIVITY

ACTIVITY 14 Human rights history quiz

Answers

Slavery and child workers

1. Free, have power to act as they wish
2. Anti-Slavery International
3. Emancipate
4. They worked in factories
5. True
6. Poverty
7. Convention on the Rights of the Child; Universal Declaration of Human Rights; Convention on the Abolition of Slavery

The Holocaust and conflict

1. Holocaust
2. Six
3. Anne Frank
4. There are more than three. Teachers can decide if those chosen are appropriate
5. Die, are killed, suffer, starve, are injured, made homeless, forced to flee....
6. Atomic
7. Refugees

Equal rights

1. Suffragette
2. Convention on the Elimination of all Forms of Discrimination Against Women
3. Apartheid
4. Nelson Mandela
5. Discriminate
6. All are human; have abilities, needs... If we all share, need to be able to secure equality, can make a contribution to the community...
7. False

International organisations

1. United Nations
2. Universal Declaration of Human Rights
3. Convention on the Rights of the Child
4. Convention
5. War crimes
6. (At time of writing) Mary Robinson
7. There are a great many. Teachers can decide if those given are appropriate

Source: Alison Gurden, with additional material from Dr Margherita Rendel.

Photocopy original © Amnesty International UK

LIVERPOOL HOPE UNIVERSITY
SHEPPARD - WORLOCK LIBRARY

3: Information and Resources

The Universal Declaration of Human Rights 1948

(Simplified version by Amnesty International UK)

Article 1
We are all born free. We all have our own thoughts and ideas. We shall all be treated in the same way. We shall treat each other with respect.

Article 2
These rights belong to everybody, whatever our differences.

Article 3
We all have the right to life, and to live in freedom and safety.

Article 4
Nobody has any right to make us a slave and we cannot make anyone else our slave.

Article 5
Nobody has the right to hurt us or to torture us.

Article 6
We all have the same right to use the law.

Article 7
The law is the same for everyone. It must treat us all fairly.

Article 8
We can all ask for the law to help us when we are not fairly treated and to give us a remedy.

Article 9
Nobody has the right to put us in prison without good reason, to keep us there or to send us away from our country.

Article 10
If we are put on trial, this should be in public.
The people who try us should not let anyone tell them what to do.

Article 11
Nobody should be blamed for doing something until it is proved. When people say we did a bad thing we have the right to show that it is untrue.

Article 12
Nobody should try to harm our good name. Nobody has the right to come into our home, open our letters, or bother us or our family without good reason.

Article 13
We all have the right to go wherever we want in our own country and travel abroad if we wish.

Article 14
If we are frightened or badly treated in our own country, we all have the right to emigrate to another country for our own safety.

Article 15
We all have the right to citizenship of a country.

Photocopy original © Amnesty International UK

The Universal Declaration of Human Rights 1948 (cont)

(Simplified version by Amnesty International UK)

Article 16
Every adult has the right to marry and have a family if they wish. Men and women have the same rights when they are married as well as before, during and after marriage.

Article 17
Everyone has the right to own things or share them. Nobody should take our possessions from us without a good reason.

Article 18
We all have the right to believe in whatever we wish, to have a faith and to change this if we wish.

Article 19
We all have the right to make up our own minds, to think what we like, and say what we think, as well as to share our ideas with other people.

Article 20
We all have the right to meet our friends and to work together in peace to defend our rights. Nobody can make us join a group if we don't want to.

Article 21
We all have the right to take part in the government of our country. All adults should be allowed to choose the leaders of their country and their representatives.

Article 22
We all have the right to a home, enough money to live on, and medical help if we are ill. Music, art and craft, and sport should be for everyone to enjoy.

Article 23
Every adult has the right to a job, to a fair wage for their work and to join a trade union and choose what work they do.

Article 24
We all have the right to rest from our work, to relax and have holidays.

Article 25
We all have the right to enjoy a good life. Mothers, children, the elderly, the unemployed and the disabled have the right to be cared for.

Article 26
Education is a right, and primary school should be free. We should learn about the UN and how to co-operate with others. Our parents may choose our education.

Article 27
We all have the right to our own way of life, and to enjoy the good things that science and learning can bring. We all can enjoy rewards from literature and artistic work.

Article 28
There must be political order and stability so that we can all enjoy rights and freedom not only in our own country but worldwide.

Article 29
We all have a duty to other people and we should protect their rights and freedom.

Article 30
Nobody can take away these rights and freedoms from us.

Photocopy original © Amnesty International UK

Convention on the Rights of the Child 1989

Some key provisions

Article 1
A child is a person under 18 years of age.

Article 2
All the rights in the convention apply to all children regardless of race, colour, sex, language, religion, political or other opinion, national, ethnic or social origin, property, disability, birth or other status.

Article 3
All decisions concerning the child should be in her/his best interests.

Article 4
States are obliged to translate the rights of the Convention into reality.

Article 6
Every child has the right to life.

Article 7
Every child has the right to a name and a nationality and as far as possible, the right to know and to be cared for by her/his parents.

Article 8
Every child has the right to protection of her/his identity by the state.

Article 9
Every child has the right to live with her/his parents unless incompatible with her/his best interests. A child who does not live with her/his parents has the right to contact with both parents.

Article 12
All children have the right to express their opinions and be heard.

Article 13
Every child has the right to express views, and obtain and transmit ideas and information regardless of frontiers.

Article 14
A child has the right to freedom of religion.

Article 15
Every child has the right to meet together with other children and to join and form associations.

Article 16
Every child must be protected from interference with privacy, family, home or correspondence.

Article 17
Children, particularly minorities, should have access to different sources of information.

Article 18
Normally, parents are responsible for bringing up their children.

Article 19
Every child has the right to protection from all forms of physical and mental violence and abuse.

Photocopy original © Amnesty International UK

Convention on the Rights of the Child 1989

Some key provisions (continued)

Article 21
A child who has no parents should be protected by the state. The child may be adopted if it is in her/his best interests.

Article 22
Children who are refugees have the right to appropriate protection and help.

Article 23
Children with disabilities have the right to special care, education and training to help them enjoy a full and active life in society.

Article 24
Every child has the right to the highest possible standard of health and medical care.

Article 27
Every child has the right to a standard of living adequate for her/his physical, mental, spiritual, moral and social development.

Article 28
Every child has the right to education, including free primary education.

Article 29
Education should develop the child's personality and talents, and respect human rights and the culture and values of the child's country.

Article 30
Children who belong to a minority race, religion or language, have the right to enjoy their own culture, practise their own religion and use their own language.

Article 31
Every child has the right to rest and leisure, and to play.

Article 32
Every child has the right to protection from economic exploitation and work that interferes with her/his education or harms her/his health or development.

Article 33
Every child has the right to protection from narcotic drugs and from being involved in their production or distribution.

Article 34
Every child has the right to protection from sexual exploitation and abuse.

Article 37
Children must not be tortured.

Article 39
The state should help children who are victims of exploitation, torture or armed conflict.

Article 40
Every child has the right, if accused or guilty of committing an offence, to be treated with care and respect.

Article 43
The convention has established a committee to oversee the implementation of children's rights.

Photocopy original © Amnesty International UK

International Convention on the Elimination of All Forms of Discrimination Against Women 1979

Some key provisions

Article 1
Discrimination against women is defined as distinction, exclusion or restrictions based on sex.

Article 2
The principle of equality between women and men.

Article 2
Women have the right, as do men, to be protected by the courts.

Article 3
States must assure the full development and progress of women. Women have the right to have and exercise the same rights as men.

Article 5
Eliminate the idea that women are inferior to men.

Article 6
Put an end to the trafficking of women and the exploitation of women through prostitution.

Article 7
Eliminate discrimination against women in political and public life. Assure this right equally with men. Assure their eligibility and ability to vote in all elections. Women have the right to participate in the political life of the state.

Article 9
Women, like men, have the right to change and to keep their nationality.

Article 10
Women have the right to the same education as men, the right of access to the same studies and to choose their future career.

Article 11
Women have the same rights to employment as men; the right to the same salary and promotion opportunities as men in the same job.

Article 11
After the birth of children, women have the right to paid maternity leave.

Article 12
Women have the right to equal access to health care.

Photocopy original © Amnesty International UK

International Convention on the Elimination of All Forms of Discrimination Against Women 1979

Some key provisions (continued)

Article 13
Women have the right to participate in all aspects of life such as playing sport, borrowing money from a bank and so on.

Article 14
Women who live in the countryside are also protected by this convention.

Article 15 (1)
Equality of women with men before the law.

Article 15 (2)
Women have the right to sign contracts and to lodge complaints against others.

Article 15 (3)
Women have the right to go where they wish and to choose their home.

Article 16
Women have the same rights as men in marriage. A woman can choose if she marries, who her husband is and she can educate her children.

Article 17
The convention has established a committee to oversee that discrimination against women is eliminated.

Version by Floriane Pettiloud (AIUK)

Photocopy original © Amnesty International UK

International Convention on the Elimination of All Forms of Racial Discrimination 1966

Some key provisions

- This convention promotes and encourages universal respect for and observance of human rights and fundamental freedoms for all, without distinction as to race, sex, language or religion.
- The term 'racial discrimination' means any distinction, exclusion, restriction or preference based on race, colour, descent, or national or ethnic origin.
- States Parties particularly condemn racial segregation and apartheid and all propaganda and all organisations based on ideas or theories of superiority of one race or group of persons of one colour or ethnic origin are prohibited.
- All human beings have the same rights. They must all be protected in the same way by law against any discrimination.

Article 5 (b)
Everybody, without distinction, has the right to be protected against violence.

Article 5 (c)
Everybody, without distinction, has the right to participate in elections.

Article 5 (d) (i)
Everybody, without distinction, has the right to freedom of movement and residence.

Article 5 (a)
Everybody, without distinction, has the right to equality before the courts.

Article 5 (d) (ii)
Everybody, without distinction, has the right to leave any country.

Article 5 (d) (iii)
Everybody, without distinction, has the right to a nationality.

Article 5 (d) (iv)
Everybody, without distinction, has the right to marriage and the choice of spouse.

Article 5 (d) (v)
Everybody, without distinction, has the right to own property.

Photocopy original © Amnesty International UK

International Convention on the Elimination of All Forms of Racial Discrimination 1966

Some key provisions (continued)

Article 5 (d) (vi)
Everybody, without distinction, has the right to inherit.

Article 5 (d) (vii)
Everybody, without distinction, has the right to freedom of thought, conscience and religion.

Article 5 (d) (viii)
Everybody, without distinction, has the right to freedom of opinion and expression.

Article 5 (d) (ix)
Everybody, without distinction, has the right to freedom of peaceful assembly and association.

Article 5 (e) (i)
Everybody, without distinction, has the right to work.

Article 5 (e) (ii)
Everybody, without distinction, has the right to form and join trade unions.

Article 5 (e) (iii)
Everybody, without distinction, has the right to housing.

Article 5 (e) (iv)
Everybody, without distinction, has the right to public health.

Article 5 (e) (v)
Everybody, without distinction, has the right to education and training.

Article 5 (e) (vi)
Everybody, without distinction, has the right to participate in cultural activities.

- States have to set up tribunals to hear complaints about racial discrimination. (Article 6)
- States should have programmes of teaching, education, culture and information to combat racial discrimination and to promote understanding. (Article 7)
- The convention has established a committee to monitor how states respect the provisions of this convention (Article 8).

Photocopy original © Amnesty International UK

Glossary

An explanation of key human rights terms in this book in simple English

abolitionist
a person or organisation who tries to put an end to a particular practice (eg to abolish slavery)

citizen
a member of a country, state or commonwealth

colonialism
a policy in which a country rules other nations and develops trade for its own benefit

concentration camp
a detention centre for political prisoners or civilians (eg as in the Boer War, World War II)

conscientious objector
a person who refuses to do something because of his/her conscience (often applied to refusing to do military service)

constitution
a system of laws which lays down how a country should be governed

covenant/convention
a treaty, convention, agreement between states that is legally binding on those that ratify it; an agreement between states; a treaty

declaration
an announcement by governments that they agree to something (eg the Universal Declaration of Human Rights)

democracy
a form of government where the power rests with the people as a whole, and where decisions are taken by a majority

democratic
allowing everyone to take part in running a country or an organisation

disabled
someone with a physical, sensory or mental impairment that seriously affects their daily lives

discriminate
to treat one group of people less fairly than another on the basis of race, age, disability, sex (eg unfair treatment of women)

economic exploitation
having to work to earn money for someone without receiving enough yourself

economy
the wealth and resources of a country

equal
having the same rights (eg suffragists wanted women to have an equal right to vote)

global
worldwide, total (often used about international economics, atmospheric warming, international conflict)

Gypsy
a member of a travelling people, sometimes also known as Romany, Roma or Sinti

holocaust
wholesale destruction by fire; usually used to refer to the mass murder of Jews in World War II

homosexual
a person attracted to members of the same sex (also known as gay or lesbian)

human rights
rights that belong to all (eg the rights in the UDHR)

industrialisation
when a society moves to working with machines

justice
fairness (eg people who bring a case at court want to see 'justice being done')

law
the rules by which a community, state or country lives by, saying what can and can't be done

moral
concerned with right and wrong (eg 'is it immoral not to treat people equally?')

Nazi
belonging to the National Socialist Workers' Party in Germany, led by Adolf Hitler

NGO
short for non-governmental organisation – a voluntary body

pacifist
a person who does not use violence under any circumstances

persecution
seriously unfair treatment of someone, normally on the grounds of their political or religious belief, race or sex

prejudice
a bias or belief, usually wrong because it is based on poor evidence or wrong assumptions (eg 'women are weak')

protocol
an agreement that adds to an international treaty

public freedoms
freedoms guaranteed and protected by the state

racism
the belief that some people are superior to others because of their ethnic descent

ratification
the approval of a treaty, convention or other document by a state

refugee
a person who has been forced to leave their home, normally because of war or natural disaster

resolution
a text agreed by an organisation (for example, by the United Nations General Assembly)

revolution
a drastic change in a government or social order (eg the Industrial Revolution)

slave
a person who is the property of another and is forced to obey her/his owner

stereotype
an over-simplified idea about a particular person or thing that is (wrongly) believed common to all (eg 'he doesn't fit the stereotype of a Muslim')

suffragette
a woman who supports the right of women to vote (eg Emmeline Pankhurst)

United Nations
the international organisation of the countries of the world set up in 1945 to promote peace and security

universal
belonging to or done by all (eg the rights in the UDHR)

violation
breaking a law, a treaty or an agreement (eg killing is a violation of the right to life)

Photocopy original © Amnesty International UK

Some organisations that work on human rights

Amnesty International UK
99-119 Rosebery Avenue
London EC1R 4RE

Anti-Slavery International
Unit 4 Stableyard
Broomgrove Road
London SW9 9TL

Bar Human Rights Committee
10-11 Gray's Inn Square
London WC1R 5JD

British Council
Bridgewater House
58 Whitworth Street
Manchester M1 6BB

British Institute of Human Rights (BIHR)
Kings College
London SE1 7AW

Centre for Citizenship Studies in Education (CCSE)
School of Education
University of Leicester
21 University Road
Leicester LE1 7RF

Centre for Global Education
College of York St John
Lord Mayor's Walk
York YO31 7EX

Charter 88
18a Victoria Park Square
London E2 9PB

Children's Legal Centre
University of Essex
Wivenhoe Park
Colchester
Essex CO4 3SQ

Children's Rights Office
319 City Road
LONDON
EC1V 1LJ

Citizenship Foundation
Ferroners House
Shaftesbury Place
off Aldersgate
London EC2Y 8AA

Commission for Racial Equality (CRE)
Elliot House
10-12 Allington Street
London SW1E 5EH

Council for Education in World Citizenship
Sir John Lyon House
5 High Timber Street
London EC4V 3NS

Development Education Association (DEA)
Third Floor
29-31 Cowper Street
London EC2A 4AT

Equal Opportunities Commission
Overseas House
Quay Street
Manchester M3 3HN

Human Rights Centre
University of Essex
Wivenhoe Park
Colchester CO4 3SQ

Minority Rights Group
379 Brixton Road
London SW9 7DE

1990 Trust
Winchester House
Room 12
9 Cranmer Road
Kennington Park
London SW9 6EJ

Quaker Peace and Social Witness
Education Advisory Programme
Friends House
Euston Road
London NW1 2BJ

Refugee Council
Bondway House
3-9 Bondway
London SW8 1SJ

Runnymede Trust
133 Aldersgate Street
London EC1A 4JA

Save the Children UK (SCUK)
17 Grove Lane
London SE5 8RD

UNICEF UK
64-78 Kingsway
London WC2B 6NB

Women's International League for Peace and Freedom
87 Turnpike Lane
Park Hill
CroydonCR0 5NU

Photocopy original © Amnesty International UK

Useful human rights websites

Amnesty International – UK	www.amnesty.org.uk
Anti-Slavery International	www.antislavery.org
Anne Frank Educational Trust (AFET)	www.annefrank.org.uk
The British Council	www.britishcouncil.org/governance
Charter 88	www.charter88.org.uk
Citizen 21	www.citizen21.org.uk
Citizenship Foundation	www.citfou.org.uk
Comic Relief	www.comicrelief.com/education
Commission for Racial Equality	www.cre.gov.uk/
Human Rights Education Associates	www.hrea.org
Human Rights Watch	www.hrw.org
Institute for Citizenship	www.citizen.org.uk
International Labour Organisation (ILO)	www.ilo.org
Runnymede Trust	www.runnymedetrusr.org/
Shelter	www.shelter.org.uk
UK Justice	www.leeds.ac.uk/law/ccjs/ukweb-2.htm
UNESCO	www.unesco.org/whc
UNESCO ASP Project	www.education.unesco.org/edwcprog/asp
UN High Commission for Human Rights (UNHCHR)	www.unhchr.ch
UN High Commissioner for Refugees (UNHCR)	www.unhcr.ch
UNICEF UK	www.unicef.org.uk

Useful history websites

University of Minnesota Human Rights Center	www.amnesty-usa.org/education
Aegis-Genocide Prevention Research Initiative	www.aegistrust.org
Anti-Nazi League	www.anl.org.uk
Benenson, Peter	www.amnesty.org.uk/amnesty/history/shtml
Beth Shalom Holocaust Centre	www.bethshalom.com
de las Casas, Bartolomé	www.hartford-hwp.com/archives/43/025.html www.campus.northpark.edu/history/webChron/Americas/DelasCasas.html
Dunant, Henri	www.nobel.se/peace/laureates/1901/dunant-bia.html
Frank, Anne	www.j1.ven.org/venSearch
Gandhi, Mahatma	www.engagedpage.com/gan1.html
Holocaust articles	www.guardianunlimited.co.uk/ Archive/Article/0,4273,4025473,00.html www.guardianunlimited.co.uk/ Archive/Article/0,4273,3927499,00.html
Holocaust Educational Trust	www.het.org.uk
Holocaust Memorial Day	www.holocaustmemorialday.gov.uk
Holocaust Exhibition	www.iwm.org.uk/lambeth/holoc-ex.htm
Holocaust publications	www.holocaustbookstore.net
Jebb, Eglantyne	www.savethechildren.org.uk/functions/aboutus/history3.html
Roosevelt, Eleanor	www.wic.org/bio/roosevel.htm
Truth, Sojourner	www.discover.net/~dansyr/truth.html
Simon Wiesenthal Centre	www.wiesenthal.com

Photocopy original © Amnesty International UK

Resources

Adams, Farrow, Jones, *Freedom!*
(Amnesty International UK/Hodder and Stoughton Educational, 2000)
Human rights education pack with materials and activities on human rights, genocide, democracy, and women's rights in history and the present day.

Anti-Slavery International, *The Changing Face of Slavery*
(Anti-Slavery International, 1998)
A video and education pack which explores the slave trade, child labour and human rights.

Anti-Slavery International, *When Rights are Left – History*
(Anti-Slavery International, 2001)
Brief 12-page notes on slavery for KS3.

Tony Bayfield, *Churban – The Murder of the Jews of Europe*
(Michael Goulston Educational Foundation, 1981)
A thoughtful study of the Holocaust written for Jewish teenagers.

Charter 88, *Have I the Right?*
(Charter 88, 1998)
Pack examining the Human Rights Act and its implications for young people in the UK.

Martin Gilbert, *The Holocaust*
(Fontana, 1989)
Masterly study of the Nazi genocide.

Reg Grant, *Talking Points – Genocide*
(Wayland Books/Amnesty International, 1998)
Well-illustrated young people's reader on genocides.

Jean Holder and Katherine Milcoy, *'Dare to be Free' and Justice at the Door! The Struggle for Women's Equality (1830–1930)* (Fawcett Library, 1997)
Pack with teacher's notes, images and texts on women in the UK – the vote, marriage and work.

N. Morgan, *Famous Campaigners for Change*
(Wayland Books, 1995)
Includes brief profiles of women human rights activists.

Peace Child International, *Stand up for Your Rights*
(Peace Child International/Two Can Publishing, 1998)
Young people write about human rights around the world.

South Yorkshire Development Education Centre, *Colonialism, Slavery and the Industrial Revolution 1700–1860*
(South Yorkshire Development Education Centre, 1992)
Education pack for KS3 with poster, two teacher's books of background and activities.

Spiro Institute, *Lessons of the Holocaust*
(Spiro Institute, 1997)
Education pack with video, teacher's notes and reproduced documents.

Kay Stearman, *When Rights are Left – Citizenship*
(Talking Points Series, 2000)
Slavery today.

Kay Stearman, *Women's Rights – changing attitudes 1900–2000* (Wayland Books/Amnesty International, 1999)
Useful background reader on women's rights.

Carrie Supple, *From Prejudice to Genocide, learning about the Holocaust* (Trentham Books, 1993)
Invaluable source material for education work on history of anti-Semitism, gypsies in the Nazi period – collaboration, indifference, dehumanisation – and other recent genocides.

Photocopy original © Amnesty International UK

550327

Index

Photocopy original © Amnesty International UK